There's No Business Like
YOUR OWN BUSINESS

VIKING
75 years

There's No Business Like
YOUR OWN BUSINESS

THE SIX PRACTICAL AND HOLISTIC

STEPS FOR ENTREPRENEURIAL SUCCESS

✦

Gladys Edmunds

Viking

VIKING
Published by the Penguin Group
Penguin Putnam Inc., 375 Hudson Street,
New York, New York 10014, U.S.A.
Penguin Books Ltd, 27 Wrights Lane, London W8 5TZ, England
Penguin Books Australia Ltd, Ringwood, Victoria, Australia
Penguin Books Canada Ltd, 10 Alcorn Avenue, Toronto,
Ontario, Canada M4V 3B2
Penguin Books (N.Z.) Ltd, 182–190 Wairau Road, Auckland 10,
New Zealand

Penguin Books Ltd, Registered Offices: Harmondsworth,
Middlesex, England

First published in 2000 by Viking Penguin, a member of
Penguin Putnam Inc.

1   3   5   7   9   10   8   6   4   2

LIBRARY OF CONGRESS CATALOGING-IN-PUBLICATION DATA
Edmunds, Gladys.
There's no business like your own business / Gladys Edmunds.
p.   cm.
ISBN 0-670-88734-X
1. Small business—Management. 2. Small business—United
States—Management.
3. Self-employed. I. Title.
HD62.7.E337 2000   99–046663
658.02'2 21—dc21

This book is printed on acid-free paper. ⊗

Printed in the United States of America
Set in ITC Century Book
Designed by Betty Lew

For my daughter, Sharon,
and
granddaughters, Stephanie and Casey

ACKNOWLEDGMENTS

First, thanks and appreciation to the many clients, staff members, and friends who continue to support my entrepreneurial endeavors of more than thirty-five years.

Special thanks and appreciation to Wesley Neff, my exceptional agent and friend, for his vision and for seeing the project through.

Gratitude and thanks to Jane von Mehren, Viking's editor extraordinaire, for sharing the vision and giving excellent editorial attention and crafting the manuscript into a better and more readable book. My sincere appreciation to her staff and coworkers: editorial assistant Jessica Kipp, whose warm and caring manner made her a welcome voice to hear from, and editor Sarah Baker for giving shape to the first draft of the manuscript while teaching me the true meaning of the word *context*. Thanks to the many people behind the scenes at Viking who worked to make this book possible.

My warmest thanks and appreciation to Helen Baynes, my sister, for sharing aspects of her life with me and allowing me to include them in this book, and to Narendra Rathore, my yoga teacher, who made a unique contribution by pointing me in the direction of finding bliss and balance as an entrepreneur.

Thanks to my mentor, confidante, and dear friend Cecile Springer, who helps and reminds me to remain objective.

What would life be like without good friends who offer suggestions and know the exact time to give moral support? My thanks and blessings to B. J. Leber, Claudia Hussein, George and Janet Miles, and Lorraine Capozzi.

Special thanks to Joy Walk, Dean Rinella, and Jackey Collier for applying their skills, talents, and technical assistance to help me meet my deadlines.

My heartfelt thanks to Asha Merlina for her assistance in the office and providing help with far too many things to list, and Tris Ozark, my assistant for ten years, for her steady work at keeping me organized.

I am especially grateful to my daughter and her family for their continued love and support and allowing me to share parts of their life with the readers. Thank you Rocky, Sharon, Stephanie, Casey, and Zoe Jackson.

And with love and gratitude my greatest thanks go to Arthur, my best friend, counselor, and husband, for his belief in me and his support, patience, and encouragement for seventeen years.

CONTENTS

Chapter Five: Achieving Balance

Chapter Six: Expanding Your Horizons

Conclusion   206

Every day I made it a point to catch the afternoon TV programs. I wasn't as interested in the shows as I was the Buster Brown shoe commercial. I positioned my twelve-year-old self in front of that tube, mesmerized, envisioning myself on the first day back to school wearing a brand-new pair of black-and-white Buster Brown saddle shoes. Even though my parents said that we couldn't afford them, I had my heart set on those shoes. I begged and pleaded, but my mother just said no. I realized that the only way I was going to get new shoes was if I bought them myself.

With school set to open in only two weeks, there wasn't enough time or baby-sitting jobs to make the money I needed for the shoes. I had to act quickly. My mother had never worked outside the home, so I knew I was stretching it when I suggested that maybe *she* might want to get a job so that she could buy my new shoes! Mom suggested that I might want to go outside and play, since I was starting to get on her nerves. But I was determined to have those shoes, so cautiously, without wanting her to blow her fuse, I asked her whether, if I figured out a way to get the money for the shoes, she would allow me to have them. I think she thought that I would call my grandparents for the money. With five other children to care for, my mother didn't have time to think about what she was agreeing to. She simply said yes.

Money was "tight" while I was growing up, and many of my family members, including my father, often found themselves looking for second jobs to make ends meet. I figured that I could help them and still get those Buster Browns. Fortunately, my voice was mature for my age, or at least I thought so. I reached for the Yellow Pages and began calling local businesses in search of work. I identified myself as a woman looking for office-cleaning jobs in order to buy back-to-school clothes for my kids and succeeded in lining up a number of prospects. My mother was shocked to find out what I had done; my father was delighted. He boasted: "Workin' ain't ever hurt nobody; in fact, it's good for the soul!"

When I closed the deals with the various business owners, my mother, father, other relatives, and neighbors would take over and do the actual cleaning, paying me a "finder's fee" for landing the contract. I had become a pint-sized businesswoman operating an employment service. My family made some extra money, and I got my shoes!

That was my first venture into the entrepreneurial world. Little did I know that three years later, with all of the so-called odds against me—teenage, black, and pregnant—the memory of that Buster Brown experience would guide me in starting my own business.

Thus began my journey as an entrepreneur, organizing and managing my own businesses and my own life. Having become an entrepreneur out of necessity, my career has lead me along a path that includes developing my own successful travel business and receiving both national and local awards for my accomplishments. I was given Avon's Women of Enterprise Award and was recognized by the Pennsylvania Department of Commerce for owning one of the Top 25 Women-Owned Businesses in the Commonwealth. I've had the opportunity to make guest appearances on *The Oprah Winfrey Show* and *Good Morning America*, and have been featured in *Money Magazine's Money Guide* and *Entrepreneur* magazine, among others, to share my story and my philosophy.

The travel company that I started more than thirty years ago is now owned by Sharon, my daughter. And my entrepreneurial life continues as president of the Gladys Edmunds Programs. The company is designed to provide motivational and inspirational support to entrepreneurs through workshops, seminars, lectures, and retreats. The purpose of this book is to share with you my blueprint for success in business and in life.

My quest for saddle shoes shaped my life forever. When I was told that I couldn't have the shoes, I became even more determined to get them. Although the word *entrepreneur* was not in my vocabulary at that time, I quickly became one. I realized that earning my own money gave me a feeling of pride and accomplishment. I also discovered that money can ease many of life's burdens for ourselves and others.

When I became pregnant at the age of fifteen, my intense determination to provide support for the baby and my desire to be a good mother made me realize that the future for both of us was in my hands. I could either choose to take control of my life, or I could live a life of uncertainty. The same energy that had driven me three years earlier emerged again. Out of desperation and will, I started on the entrepreneurial journey that would shape the rest of my life.

During the years that I worked to succeed in business I grew, too. And not just economically, but emotionally, mentally, and spiritually. I came to understand that the principles required for running a successful business are also applicable in one's personal life. My greatest realization was that life is not composed of unconnected segments—the economic life, the emotional life, the spiritual life, the parental life, etc.—but is the sum total of them all. If one part is out of balance, then the whole is disrupted. No single piece should become more powerful than the whole. I believe in living a holistic life in which we deal with our life as a whole rather than breaking it into its separate parts. It is necessary for all aspects of our life to be in balance for it, as a whole, to be successful and fulfilling. If life is lived holistically, there will be no concern about being a good parent, friend, or entrepreneur. All the various aspects of our being will work together to make us complete, the person that we strive to be.

I have learned many of the lessons that life has to offer an entrepreneur—often the hard way. Along the way, I have realized that the key to business success is not how well you can juggle bank loans, write a 150-page business plan, or negotiate a contract. The real key to a thriving business is how you handle and balance the many aspects of your life. My experience has shown me that if there is chaos in one aspect of your life, you can be guaranteed that there will be chaos generally. We have to listen to our inner, intuitive voice for answers to our problems and for direction in our life, whether business or personal. All of us possess this little voice. If we learn to listen to it and respond, it will help us find a solution to our difficulties. We have to learn to trust our intuition and rely on our inherent abilities to solve the dilemmas of our lives. This book will address how to do that.

The experiences in my life and the actions that I have taken, some proactive and some reactive, have taught me valuable lessons that I want to share with other entrepreneurs. I hope to help you organize and accentuate the positive in your business *and* your personal life so that you can live a balanced and holistic life. The decision that I made early in life was to live by choice and not by chance. I encourage you to do that, too.

This book is intended for three types of people: the existing entrepreneur who is ready to move to the next level of achievement; those of you who would like to own your own business; and finally, those of you who are working for a company and want a more productive life by learning how to bring the separate aspects of life into a harmonious whole. I will show you *how* to do it and not just tell you *what* to do!

The book is divided into six chapters. Each chapter represents one of the six steps that I found necessary to achieve my goals. As you journey with me, you will meet a number of people from my workshops, lectures, and retreats and some that I have met in passing. Together we will show you how these six steps can be used to achieve success. The sections contained in each chapter will offer you examples, anecdotes, stories, thoughts to think on, and insights that will help you apply these lessons to your own life, because **THERE'S NO BUSINESS LIKE YOUR OWN BUSINESS.**

THE SIX STEPS TO ENTREPRENEURIAL SUCCESS

In order to accomplish your entrepreneurial dream, you must first have a well-thought-out reason for why you want to become an entrepreneur. The methods for arriving at, understanding, and embracing it are explored through step one, **Taking Charge of Your Thoughts.** Step two, **Overcoming Obstacles,** allows you to learn how to face and deal with problems, whether internal or external, and solve them. Step three, **Establishing Communication,** helps you maximize your potential in three areas of communication vital to the entrepreneur: your business, such as marketing, sales, and advertising; the communication that must take place within us for guaranteed success; and finally, effective methods of communication with the people around us. Step four, **Building a Dynamic Support System,** shows you how to surround yourself with the right people to become a more effective and efficient entrepreneur. Step five, **Achieving Balance,** will help you create a systematic approach to nourish all areas of your life. Finally, step six, **Expanding Your Horizons,** will help you achieve the growth and empowerment needed to attain the success that you deserve.

Just as with life, any enterprise is a *process*, a series of steps toward a desired result. It doesn't always come easily; it is something that we must work at constantly and consciously to develop, just as we grow and evolve. Yet each of us, if we so desire, has the potential to make our dreams come true. It is my wish to share what I've learned with you. So let's begin that journey together.

Chapter 1

TAKING CHARGE OF YOUR THOUGHTS

✦

We will all get a wake-up call; a reality check, so to speak, at some point in our lives. Sometimes it comes early in life; often it doesn't come until much later. Sometimes the call is faint and hard to hear, but for me it came fast and furious and with a thundering sound. That was the day that I discovered, at the age of fifteen, while I was still in high school, that I had a baby on the way and no money. As the oldest child of nine from a hardworking blue-collar family, I knew there wasn't enough money to feed yet another mouth.

Daddy had quit school to work and help his mother raise twelve kids after the death of his father. As a result, he often bragged to his friends about how I would be the first person from his side of the family to graduate from high school and go to college. My mom, on the other hand, had her own plans for me. Actually, they were her own plans to live through me and reclaim her adolescence, especially the prom, which she had forfeited when she quit school in order to marry and raise a family. The cloud of disappointment over my house because of my pregnancy made it impossible for me to remain there.

Fortunately, I found shelter with my grandmother, but it was clear that my future—and my baby's—were squarely in my hands. Even at my young age, I knew my problems were my own and that they were my responsibility.

Conventional wisdom of the 1960s said that a pregnant inner-city teenager would be doomed to a life of failure. If this was the message that fate had in store for me, I wasn't aware of it. My first instinct was to find work, and fast. But each so-called employment opportunity turned into a door being slammed in my face.

In order for me to become responsible for finding solutions to my dilemma, I had to take a giant leap from being a fun-loving, carefree teen into the on-my-own, often scary world of adulthood. My brief but fruitful entrepreneurial experience three years earlier with the Buster Brown shoes proved to me that I was determined and stubborn enough to earn my own money. Yet one moment I would picture myself having everything that I needed and wanted, confident and capable in the pursuit of my goals. Then, seconds later, I would become plagued by fear and begin to feel overwhelmed, depressed, and uncertain about my abilities to succeed in taking care of my baby and myself. My tendency to vacillate back and forth forced me to take a closer look at what was happening in my head. How could I think and feel confident, positive, and ambitious one minute and be shrouded in doubt, fear, and bewilderment the next? The feelings of uncertainty that I experienced during this critical stage of my life led to the realization that I had to **TAKE CHARGE OF MY THOUGHTS.**

THOUGHTS AND THINKING

There are all kinds of thoughts that run through our minds. Some are good, some are bad, and some are neutral. Whatever category our thoughts fit into, one thing is certain: When we give them our attention, they can either empower, energize, and carry us to victory or leave us feeling afraid, uncertain, and defeated. We cannot control the parade of thoughts marching through our minds. But we can choose which ones we will give our attention to. Picture your thoughts as people passing by the front of your home. Just because they're walking by doesn't mean you have to invite them in. Merely deciding which thoughts and feelings to focus on can make the difference between whether you end up in the alleyway of failure or on the avenue to success. In other words, how we think affects how we feel, how we feel affects how we behave, and how we behave determines the outcome.

Consider for a moment why some people are financially well-heeled and others are robbing Peter to pay Paul. Some folks are happy as larks, while others seem to be wallowing in the slough of despair. There are those who are bursting with creative energy, while others are beset by inertia. Let's not forget those folks who lament their fears and doubts about being successful, yet their alter egos show steadfast confidence and self-assurance.

Why the contrast? I've asked this question of many people, and I've received all sorts of answers. A few say that some people are luckier than others. Others cite such factors as environment and social background; still others argue that it's genetic. Rarely does anyone suggest that this contrast has something to do with mind-set.

The way in which you choose to think will display itself not only in your business but in your entire being. Walk into any business and take a quick look around. You will instantly be able to see and feel the attitude, philosophy, and mission of its owner. The "thinking thoughts" of the owner are everywhere and will project themselves onto others. Let's take a look at Mary:

Mary's Story

Mary owns her own gardening and landscaping business. When she first started out, she lived in a small community and would stop at nothing to find customers for her business. She took out small classified ads in the local paper, approached people in church and at the supermarket, and nailed flyers to neighborhood telephone poles. She would even walk up to strangers performing their Saturday-afternoon grass-cutting rituals and strike up casual conversations about grass seed, tree pruning, or flower planting.

Her first year was very profitable, and she counted on things getting even better. She had an art-history degree from a major university and had worked as a college instructor. But gar-

dening was her passion, and she had struggled the previous year to finish her certification as a master gardener. She was ready for bigger and better things. Mary felt that fate was on her side when her husband received a promotion that required them to move to a larger city and live in a more upscale community. She believed that the move was just what she needed to take her business to a higher level.

Once she settled into her new neighborhood, Mary quickly went to work placing ads for her business on the radio and local cable stations. However, weeks went by, and customers weren't calling. She couldn't understand why. She began to spend more and more money on advertisements, but only a few prospects trickled in. Her husband, Tom, suggested that she go back to her "old ways" and create flyers and "cruise the neighborhood" for lawn cutters and home gardeners. But Mary felt that when she had moved into this well-to-do community, she had become much too sophisticated for that kind of soliciting.

Mary thought her luck was changing when a local newspaper reporter wanted to interview her for the Home and Garden section of the Sunday edition. The reporter asked Mary several questions about gardening and landscaping and was obviously impressed by her expertise. Mary told the reporter that she was having difficulty getting customers. "Your work is beautiful. I'm surprised more people haven't heard of you," he said. Mary remarked, "I thought that when I moved here, I was moving into a city where people were familiar with the more sophisticated methods of landscaping. But that isn't the case; I'm surprised by how backward and behind the times people here are."

Having been a resident of the city his whole life, the reporter became extremely offended. That Sunday, a far-from-flattering article about Mary's business appeared in the paper.

Mary is still baffled as to why the folks in her new community have failed to recognize the wonderful services she has to offer. Perhaps

Mary's thoughts and feelings of "eliteness" have kept her from coming into close contact with the people around her. In her old community, Mary was known; she frequently interacted with the people around her. But in her new community she has no way of knowing whether her potential customers are backward and behind the times or too high-class to want her services because Mary has never interacted with them. Most likely Mary doesn't even realize that the thoughts she's chosen to entertain about herself and the people in her new community are counterproductive to her business. This is a problem that occurs when we don't pay close attention to the thoughts we choose to "think" on. Our actions are based on our thoughts. When we are not in control of our thoughts, particularly those critical of others, we tend to say and do things that are offensive and destructive. Mary said hurtful things about the people in her community, which in turn had an adverse effect on her business. Had she recognized the connection between thoughts and actions before she spoke, her interview could have gone better and perhaps her business as well.

How do we know which thoughts to pay attention to? There are some things that we instinctively know are wrong. For example, we know that stealing is wrong because we have a code of ethics that states, "Thou shall not steal," and all of us understand that. But nowhere is it written: "Thou shall not refer to thy neighbors as backward and behind the times." And that's where the line gets thin. If Mary had examined her thoughts and separated the ones that she was *certain* were wrong from the thoughts she wasn't particularly sure of, then she could have examined her unsure thoughts from another point of view. She needed to step back and consider how such thoughts could be perceived; she needed to imagine how she would react if someone called her "backward and behind the times" or anything else that didn't fit the image she had of herself. My guess is that if Mary had done so, she would have realized just how insulting those comments can be. I believe if Mary had *known* that the thoughts she was entertaining were hurtful to her growing business, she would never have voiced them aloud—and certainly not to a reporter!

Therefore, it's critical to understand where our thoughts will lead us. Are they productive or counterproductive? We are always making choices, and it is ultimately up to us to choose which thoughts we will or will not entertain. As you can see from Mary's experience, your thoughts *will* get expressed to others and are a direct reflection of *you*. You can't allow yourself to think unflatteringly about your potential customers and still expect them to buy your services and products. Remember, your customers are human beings who like personal attention and having their needs addressed whether they live in a small working-class community or a wealthy suburb. Think of your potential clients, no matter where they live, as people who are worthy of the best. And bear in mind that a bad thought a day can keep the customer away!

The success or failure of our businesses hinges on how well we are able to control which thoughts we choose to act on. Of the thousands of thoughts that pass through our minds each day, the majority come from external stimuli: radio, television, newspapers, and idle chatter. Fortunately, like the people passing in front of our homes, most of them go by us unnoticed. But there are those that manage to get our attention. When a counterproductive thought gets my attention, I mentally repeat, Thank goodness this thought doesn't belong to me, or, Thank you for sharing, but I'm busy now and will deal with you later. Later, I do address thoughts that are nagging me. Negative thoughts can be helpful when handled properly, as you'll see later in this chapter.

For thousands of years the great yoga and meditation masters of the Far East have known the importance of exercising control over our thoughts and emotions. They say that if we can live consistently in the present moment, our minds will not wander. I believe that they are correct. However, constantly living in the present moment is sometimes easier said than done. I find it simple enough do so when I am involved in my morning yoga exercise. However, seconds after leaving the yoga mat, my mind often starts racing due to the many things that require my attention.

The good news is there are ways to stay on top of our thoughts and feelings that we can practice throughout the day. The three methods I use most are:

+ Humor. It's not hard to find something to laugh at, and finding humor in some of the contradictions in life helps me keep things in perspective. Go see a funny movie, read a funny book, or laugh at something foolish that you may have done. It's hard to laugh and think poorly at the same time.
+ Exercise! I take a brisk three-mile walk around Highland Park every morning and experience the beauty of nature. I arrive at my office feeling more alive and energized after the fresh air has cleared my mind.
+ Experience something pleasant every day. Look for it, or make something refreshing happen.

But we're all different, and you might benefit from other techniques. Try listening to uplifting music or practice deep-breathing exercises. Or do something you've always wanted to do, no matter how crazy or farfetched you think the idea might be. Take up karate, ballet, or a foreign language, or become a volunteer for a cause you truly believe in . . . and follow it through. Nothing gives you a feeling of control more than a sense of accomplishment. Take the case of my daughter, Sharon, who enrolled in a weight-lifting class shortly after the birth of her first child. Not only did she develop her biceps but also an "I can do anything" attitude. A sense of accomplishment will positively affect your thoughts and feelings.

The power of affirmations should not be underestimated. You might take a few minutes daily to do three or four deep breathing exercises, relax your body, and recite, mentally or out loud, an affirmation. It doesn't have to be anything elaborate or ritualistic, but you should follow these two rules: (1) Make certain that it is in the present tense and (2) that it is always positive. Something as simple as "I am all right right now" is good or "My business is supplying all of my financial needs." Use one or two affirmations until you feel that they have become true in your life and then move on to another. Or choose what makes you feel good. Give your affirmation added power by imagining it in your mind and project your emotions onto the image by feeling the joy and sense of accomplishment. Your mind, body, and emotions will thank you. You want to take charge of your thoughts because your thinking enables you to make important business and life decisions successfully—and instinctively. Take a look at Steve:

Steve's Story

For eight years Steve worked hard to develop his janitorial company. When he started he had only one part-time employee, and over the years he built his business into a forty-eight-employee operation. He believed that he owed his success to his ability to work hard and put in long hours. Steve thought that anything less from his employees was a sign that they had no respect for him. He required his employees to be at work on time, in uniform, and to get their orders. He had no tolerance for idle chatter between employees that didn't relate directly to their work. Sick days were tolerated only with a doctor's note. Leaving early was out of the question, and vacation wasn't allowed until an employee had been on the job for at least two years. He didn't allow personal phone calls at work, either.

One day, one of Steve's employees received a call at work telling her there was an emergency at home. Reluctantly, Steve allowed the woman to take the call, but after she had hung up, he reminded her about his rule against receiving personal calls. He believed he was a "no-nonsense" businessman. In his mind, that was the key to success.

Steve had plenty of customers, but he couldn't figure out why his profits were not greater. He spent nights poring over his books, and he was also worried about the high turnover rate of his employees.

"I don't understand it," Steve told me one day. "I hire them,

pay them on time, tell them exactly what to do each day and how to do it; they don't even have to waste time thinking on their own. Hell, I even give them uniforms!" Steve was perplexed, but wrote it off to the old adage Good help is hard to find.

One late night, Steve was struggling with his books again as he listened to a talk-radio show. The subject was "respect." Even though he was barely paying attention, Steve happened to hear: "Respect is earned, not given." All the way home, Steve couldn't get those words out of his head. The words preyed on his mind for the rest of that evening and into the night.

It was business as usual for the next few weeks. Steve's profits weren't increasing, and employees continued to leave. There were many times during those few weeks that the words "Respect is earned, not given" would unexpectedly come into Steve's mind.

One evening, while Steve was working late, one of his employees entered his office. "Hey, Steve, there's a heck of a snowstorm out there. The roads are a sheet of ice. A few of the workers are having trouble getting back in here, and there's one more job left to do. What should I tell them?"

Steve was just about to give his usual reply, "Tell 'em to just get the job done and get back in here," when the words about respect that had kept haunting him entered his head.

"Tell 'em to wait where they are. I'll get the four-wheel drive, pick them up, and bring them back to their cars. As for the one job left, if you would be willing to go along with me to that job, we can knock it out in half the time." The words came out of Steve's mouth before he could think about them. Steve was just as shocked as his employee at his response. As time went on, Steve found himself pitching in to help in areas that were understaffed. He even apologized to the employee who had received the "personal phone call" about the family emergency. At first, Steve's employees were a little suspicious of him and his newfound kindness. Some thought that his sudden "helping hand" was a novel way to keep an eye on them. But over

time they realized that Steve really was just out there to get the job done. Steve also began to notice some very subtle changes in his employees. Their attitude changed, and the atmosphere on the job went from "every man for himself" to a "we are family" approach. They began helping each other more, and some even helped Steve with the office work if he was late or pressed for time! His employees stopped leaving the company, and Steve's profits started to grow.

Word got out that Steve had become a pretty decent guy to work for, and a steady stream of people began to apply for work. Not only had Steve's new approach solved his bottom-line problem—employee turnover—but it resulted in an opportunity for him to grow his business.

Steve's original attitude toward his employees and his turnaround are so dramatic that it is almost unbelievable. But they are a good illustration of what happens when we don't pay close attention to our *thinking* thoughts.

"Respect is earned" is not a novel insight, but like a seed, it was planted in Steve's thought patterns and remained there. Allow good thoughts to take root in your mind. Nourish them. Give them ample room for growth. Don't force them and you will be surprised at the results. Like a seed, good thoughts will slowly take root, sprout, and flower into something beautiful.

Steve picked up on the thought "Respect is earned, not given" and played it over and over in his mind until it became his mantra. Become more aware of which thoughts are beneficial to you and which are not. You can't always keep a constant vigil over your thoughts, but it will help you if you make a conscious effort.

✦ THOUGHT TO THINK ON ✦

There is an old African proverb that states, "A needle cannot hold two threads or a mind two thoughts."

Insights into Thoughts

1. Use your thoughts to your best advantage.
2. Rise above distracting thoughts by saying mentally or aloud, "Thank goodness this thought doesn't belong to me."
3. Thoughts need your energy (attention) to have an effect on your life. Put concentration and action behind your good thoughts.

PURPOSE: LIFE'S MAIN MOTIVATOR

Even though doubts regularly enter our minds, our *will* can defeat them. Perseverance, determination, and faith are fueled by our sense of purpose; our purpose is the reason why we do what we do. What is your purpose? Why did you get out of bed this morning? Was it because you have a business and your customers, clients, and employees expect you to show up? Maybe you were forced out of bed by hungry kids, a full bladder, or a dog badly in need of its morning walk.

Any of the above is certainly a motivating factor in getting out of bed, but what was the greater reason that caused you to rise and start another day? What do you feel an unending commitment to and a great passion for? Your ultimate purpose is that special something that is born of your determination and commitment. Figuring out, knowing, and living by your ultimate purpose will help you meet your goals in life. Only when you identify it can you find your motivation.

Your purpose is your catalyst—that substance that increases the rate at which a chemical reaction takes place. Let's look at the chemical makeup of water, H_2O. If we were to combine two atoms of hydrogen and one atom of oxygen, one would think that the result would be water. Not so. Something has to be added to the mix in order to produce that result. In the case of H_2O, the catalyst is some form of energy; that is, a spark of fire, compression of hot air, or a charge of electricity is necessary in order for the hydrogen and oxygen to produce water.

My ultimate purpose in life was to make a good life for my daughter. I wanted to create an environment that would not only be encouraging, nurturing, and financially secure for her but would allow her to look up to, respect, and admire me. During the early days of the 1960s, I would often hear people referring to the children of unmarried women as illegitimate, impure, or misbegotten, and believe me, those weren't the worst words that were used. I made a commitment to myself that no one would ever refer to my child in such a negative way. I kept that in mind as I moved through life, developing myself and my business.

For me, my daughter was my main purpose. For you, it could be anything, from wealth, power, and enjoying a growing business to deciding that you want to do something good for humankind and the planet. Your ultimate purpose can be anything that you desire; it will become your motivation, a sturdy foundation that you can build on. To identify your purpose, just ask yourself, What in life is worth "busting my tail" for? What in this life is worth making a commitment from my heart to be responsible for? Purpose has a way of changing as we grow. At one point, your purpose may be the desire to have total abundance for you and your family. After you get that, your purpose may shift toward achieving something you have always wanted or be concerned with something else. Once you identify your purpose, take the next step. Embrace it; make it your life's work. After you have accomplished this, taking charge of your thoughts and focusing your attention in the right place and in the right way becomes much easier.

One of the best ways to approach a project is to see it as being new and fresh and not allow it to become stale and outdated or lose its zest. When we approach projects as if they are always new, we are more open and receptive to exploring different angles and various approaches. In Zen meditation there's a concept referred to as "beginner's mind." When we approach our projects as beginners and not as experts, we can do so with the freshness of an explorer on a pioneer expedition. The idea is to remain open to all possibilities as you move forward. Providence will take hold and guide you, opening doors and making paths visible that you never thought possible. As with anything that is new, there is always some doubt. Be thankful for it. It has a way of keeping us on our toes and not allowing us to rest on our laurels. On the other hand, we should not allow ourselves to be consumed by doubt, or we will not be able to move forward. The way to know whether a project could be beneficial to you is to try it with an alert and enthusiastic beginner's mind.

✦ THOUGHT TO THINK ON ✦

Your purpose is the catalyst that, when added to heartfelt commitment and strong-willed determination, creates a flow of success beyond your imagination.

Insights into Discovering Your Purpose

1. Write down the things in your life that you feel are important.
2. Examine them and search for the one thing that lights a fire beneath you and gives you a feeling of passion or *purpose.*
3. Once you've defined your purpose, keep it in your mind and let it guide you.

WHAT YOU FOCUS ON IS WHAT YOU GET

When our ultimate purpose is clear in our minds, we can move to the next step, *focusing.* Think of focusing as walking on a balance beam—slow and steady and concentrating all of your energy on staying on it while moving forward.

When I was seven years old, I watched an older kid from our neighborhood hold a magnifying glass over a pile of newspapers and start a fire. Of course, the other children on the block were awed and fascinated by this stunt. I tried endlessly to duplicate the feat; however, nothing happened. One day my grandfather noticed my frustration and walked over to where I was sitting, irritated, on the sidewalk. He explained that the fire wasn't igniting because I wasn't focusing the lens of the magnifying glass steadily over the newspaper in line with the sunlight. At that point, Grandpa placed his hand over mine, and we held the magnifying glass near the edge of the papers. Because of this focused action, the sun's energy was allowed to intensify through the glass, and a fire started. Needless to say, my popularity soared among the other kids. Thanks to Grandpa, I had learned the importance of being focused.

One definition of focus is "point of concentration." This is exactly where we need to be in our endeavors, at a point of concentration. It is at that *point* where we place our focus that the energy starts to accumulate.

A laser is one steady stream of light with the force of many beams of light concentrated into that one stream. This, too, is focusing. We need to think of ourselves that way when applying ourselves to our endeavors. All of our energies must be concentrated into one energy to do our best thinking, our best creating, our best decision making. It is important to learn the art of focusing and remaining focused in order to accomplish your goal. How do you learn to stay focused? Practice paying attention first; that will lead you into a concentrated focus.

Too often more time is spent focusing on our shortcomings and not enough time is spent focusing on our strong points, that is, talents, accomplishments, and skills. Understand your limitations and use them to grow.

We all remember the story of the little drummer boy. This young boy lost his home, his family, and his village due to sad and tragic circumstances. He was out on his own in the world at the very young age of twelve. He got mixed up with some pretty shady people for a while but thankfully was able to get away from them and eventually stumbled across the wise men on their way to visit the Christ child. Upon entering the stable and seeing the wise men presenting the child with very expensive gifts, he realized he had nothing of value to give to the babe. He was distraught over this and berated himself for not having something suitable for a king. "I have no gift to bring . . . that's fit to give a king," he said.

It occurred to the drummer boy, after much agonizing and soul-searching, that the only gift he could offer the child was the gift of playing his drum. Hesitantly, he began to play softly on his drum as he walked near the manger. And remember those famous last lines: "Then he smiled at me . . . me and my drum."

This song is a classic example of focusing energy on what we may be *lacking* and not realizing what we *have*. Whether in our personal lives or in our entrepreneurial endeavors, we all have a unique *something* to bring to the table. And that is where we should focus our energy: on our *strengths and uniqueness*, not our weaknesses. Every successful entrepreneur learns this lesson at one time or another. It is okay to know what our weaknesses are; learn from them, get to know them. But the trick is to use that knowledge to grow. Not one of us is going to be good at everything, but we're all good at something. Take it from the little drummer boy. Use what you have.

✦ THOUGHT TO THINK ON ✦

Don't focus on what you don't have; what you have is too valuable.

Insights into Focusing

1. Concentrate on the object of your attention.
2. When other thoughts get in the way, just allow them to float by without giving them your attention.
3. If at the beginning you find it hard to focus or concentrate, don't give up. The more you practice, the easier it will get.
4. Focusing is like walking on a balance beam. It's slow and

steady and forces all of your energy on remaining there while moving forward.

USE WHAT YOU KNOW AND START WHERE YOU ARE

Starting right now, where you are, may well mean starting with serious limitations. Many successful businesspeople started on a wing and a prayer, with no capital or business plan. What they did have was an idea. Along with their commitment, determination, imagination, and unique abilities, they developed their idea into a successful business. Sam is a good example.

Sam's Story

My friend Sam stopped by my office one day to ask a favor; he needed to borrow some money to pay off a few debts. I was in the middle of giving him my speech about "doing for yourself" and "starting your own business" when Sam interrupted me. "I don't have the money to start my own business," he interjected. "Sam," I began, "sometimes the capital for the start-up of a business only requires enough money for the purchase of a snow shovel during a day like today, when there's a snowstorm outside." Sam had no shovel or the money to buy one. So I let him borrow mine.

Taking my advice, Sam went into the snow-removal business with the intention of shoveling a few driveways and walks to make a few extra dollars. However, that winter turned out to be one of the worst that Pittsburgh had ever seen; it snowed almost every other day. Sam paid a visit to shopkeepers in the area and made arrangements to shovel their sidewalks. Many hired him to go to their homes and remove the snow, giving him an opportunity to offer his services to the homeowners in the neighborhood. A big plus came for Sam when he called on a real estate company and got a contract to keep the sidewalks free of snow in front of fifteen apartment buildings. Sam not only wound up with enough money to pay off some of his debt but was also able to purchase a pickup truck to help him in his new handyman business. And I got my shovel back!

Even though Sam thought starting a business from his station in life would be impossible, he was able to do so, exceeding his original goals.

The key is to not worry about starting small. Just start. After all, the Great Wall of China began with a single stone. Concentrate on what it is you have, and before you know it, what you have will produce more. A reporter once asked Henry Ford what he would do if he ever became bankrupt. Mr. Ford replied that he would just think of a simple idea, something people needed, and he would find a way to give it to them.

In Sam's case, a borrowed shovel during a bad winter helped him build a handyman business. In my case, at the age of twelve, a telephone and the Yellow Pages were the only tools I needed to get my much-wanted Buster Brown shoes. You don't need a hefty bank loan, a spacious office, or a secretary to start a successful business. You only need to start. Just by starting, you're that much closer to realizing your aspirations.

✦ THOUGHT TO THINK ON ✦

To be willing is to be able.

Insights into Starting Where You Are

1. Examine all the things that you are capable of doing and what you can do with them.
2. Examine all of the resources that you have at your disposal and decide how they can assist you.

3. When you find yourself saying that you "can't afford" the
   money to go into business, use that as your cue to make
   use of what you have available right here and now.

SET GOALS THAT YOU CAN SEE

Are the goals set at a great distance ever really reached? We can
reach our goals more easily if we can see them. Keep in mind the saying "From little acorns big oaks grow" as you set your goals. Keep
track of the goals that are within your reach as you accomplish them.
One day you will look back and see that you've made tremendous
progress.

I distinctly remember being in the hospital after the birth of my
daughter, Sharon. As I lay there, I listened to the other women talking about their goals and dreams for their babies' future. Back then
the hospitals would line up twelve or fourteen beds in one big, long
maternity ward. As fate would have it, I was the youngest woman
there. I'll never forget the comments of one glowing new mother as
she remarked, "The moment I saw my son, I said to myself, This is a
Harvard graduate." I recall lying there and thinking, What on earth is
Harvard? At that time I had no idea what that mother was talking
about. But the key word to me was "graduate," so I figured that it had
to be something far off into the future.

That's when I realized that my goals and dreams for my daughter's
future were much more immediate. My objectives for the future were
returning home from the hospital and buying formula and diapers.
Often I think of that other new mother and wonder if her son ever
made it to Harvard.

My goals have always been reachable, ones that I could see. As I
lay in the maternity ward, I could visualize buying diapers and formula for my baby; I couldn't foresee life eighteen years away. Buying
diapers may seem quite simplistic when compared to graduating
from an Ivy League school; however, I can say that I succeeded. I was
successful because I attacked my goals by degrees and far exceeded
my first humble expectations.

To begin setting yourself up for success, focus on the task at hand and set goals that you can realize. In most athletic games—hockey, basketball, football, tennis, soccer—players are always able to see the goal that they are trying to reach. At no point are the players *not* able to see it. So then why do we set goals that we can't see?

Eric's story will present a clearer picture of what happens when we can see our goals:

Eric's Story

Eric, an ex–vice president of marketing for a large corporation, came to me seeking advice. Downsized three times by the time he was thirty years old, he couldn't take it anymore. He decided he wanted to go into business for himself. First, he bought a "how to start your own business" book and over a four-month period concocted an elaborate, 150-page business plan! Eric's goal was to start his own marketing and public-relations company directed toward the health-care world. He wanted me to help him find a lending institution to finance his business. According to the business plan, he would need to borrow $500,000 to just get the business started! Eric's business plan overflowed with executive details.

I began by getting Eric over the fact that he would no longer have a private secretary, a plush private office, a travel expense account, a team of employees who were sitting around waiting to turn his ideas into reality, or any of the other perks of his previous positions. You see, Eric saw himself having all the perks of his past positions (a goal too distant to reach) at the start of his new business venture. Eric didn't think he could start a business without all of those other things in place.

I asked Eric, "What do you have now?" He replied, "Nothing." And that is where we started, with nothing.

Eric didn't even own a computer at the time—he had typed his business plan at a neighborhood copy center. I told him to go back to the copy center and type a good sales and promotional letter to distribute to area businesses. What he really needed to get started were customers. *"Eric," I said, "put away that business plan and sell what you* know, *not what those books are telling you that you should know. And look at the things in your business plan as your long-term goal and work with short-range goals that you can see." I also suggested that he purchase a pager with a voice-mail message from him to potential customers; this would allow him to appear as if he* did *have an office. The pager gave him the ability to receive messages and return phone calls promptly without the expense of an office and secretary. Nobody would know or care that his was a one-man operation, provided he served his clients quickly, efficiently, and above all, professionally. With the way technology is designed today, it is difficult to distinguish between a larger business and a smaller one.*

It took several months, but Eric did it. He began his marketing and PR business with one company: a nursing home. Soon he was referred to others. Eric was on his way to successful entrepreneurship. Today Eric has a thriving clientele, works from his home, and makes more money than he did at his previous jobs.

Early in my career I read a newspaper story that taught me the significance of being able to see the goal one is trying to reach.

Every year, on New Year's Day, a Florida woman hired a boat to take her several miles out in the Atlantic Ocean, and to celebrate another year of life, she swam back to shore. It was her own personal tradition. The boat stayed nearby so that she could bail out if she ran out of energy, but she never did. On one particular January 1, there was a heavy fog, so heavy that she couldn't see the shoreline (her goal). Partway in, she was laboring hard, and finally she was so exhausted that she had to give up. After she was helped into the boat, she was shocked to find that she was just twenty yards from shore.

It's been more than twenty-five years since I read that story, but I've never forgotten it, and I always make certain that my goals are ones that I can see.

✦ THOUGHT TO THINK ON ✦

What we call results are beginnings.

—Ralph Waldo Emerson

Insight into Goals You Can See

1. Concentrate on the immediate task at hand.
2. It's the small things you accomplish in the beginning that build confidence and pave the way for greater prosperity.
3. Take a "do it now" attitude. You won't get far if you wait to have everything you need.

NEGATIVE THOUGHTS: THE POWER PATH

Negative thoughts also need to be embraced. We have to address that which might hold us back or stunt our growth so that we can move forward. For example, if your thought is I'm never going to meet this goal, stop and investigate that attitude. There is merit in the idea that we should replace a negative thought with a positive one, but be careful. This school of thought can also be self-defeating unless we take the time to see how we can use it to our best advantage. Looking at negative thoughts and attitudes straight on instead of trying to push them aside will allow us to eventually overcome them and move ahead.

Examining feelings and thoughts of uncertainty can help you know yourself better. Ask yourself questions like Why am I feeling and thinking this way? and How do these feelings and thoughts affect my life? Where is this coming from? Don't take your negative thought, or any thought that you are uncomfortable with, and drown it by quickly trying to replace it with a positive one; sooner or later the negative one will resurface with more power than before. You must consider thoughts as problems, as you would in business. You wouldn't ignore an unsatisfied customer, would you? No. As a successful business owner you would get to the root of the problem and find a way to handle it effectively and make yourself and the customer happy. You would address the problem, resolve it, and then move on to the next order of business. It is imperative to address apprehensive and doubtful thoughts and feelings as they arise. Deal with them right away, and subsequently you will diffuse some of their power and get to know yourself better. When situations are dealt with and handled properly, we can move to the next stage of development.

We know that business can be great one day and not so great the next; that's the way life is. The beauty of the not-so-great days is the memory of the great days. Life is circular. Although today's a good day, tomorrow may not be. But once we've experienced a few successes, we know, even on bad days, that great days will come again. Even "bad" days are good. We don't grow from a string of good, easy days. We grow from the hard days, the tough days, and the bothersome things that happen to us along the way. Let's take a look at how Sally took charge of her thoughts and feelings:

Sally's Story

Sally finally did it. She was in business for herself, operating a small catering service from her home. All her life friends had told her what a great cook she was and that with her talents she should develop her own business. She was thrilled. She had already lined up a few customers and had successfully catered several small affairs in her community. Word spread, and Sally finally landed her first large project, a wedding reception at a fancy country club.

The week before the wedding, Sally was preparing the desserts when a huge cloud of doubt settled over her.

What if I can't do this? What if they hate my food and I'm there watching them eat it and they demand to know who the chef is? What if they agree this is the worst food they've ever eaten in their lives? Sally's misgivings were endless. She couldn't shake the parade of negativity marching through her mind. Consequently, her first batch of cookies was a flop.

Sally, very upset at this point, called me to discuss her need to take control of her thoughts. After a short conversation, I suggested that Sally first calm herself down and then take a look at each disturbing thought. She started by simple deep breathing to calm her busy mind and her nerves, and then began to address each doubt.

It didn't take long for Sally to discover the origin of some of her fears. As a young girl, Sally spent her summers in New England with her Aunt Millie, an older aunt whom Sally loved and respected very much. However, Aunt Millie was an absolute perfectionist when it came to entertaining. Moreover, she believed that preparing and serving food, especially for guests, required talent. Sally would get extremely nervous when it was her turn to set the table for a family dinner. To this day, Sally could hear Aunt Millie's most famous conviction: "Cooking is a fine art, and most know it not!" Sally realized that this was the source of most of her anxiety. She would examine closely every thought she had that wasn't positive. As she identified each negative thought from some outside source, she would say aloud, "Thank God this is not my thought; it's only an intrusive thought from some other place and time."

As Sally became more comfortable, she began to entertain thoughts that were more helpful to her: This is my first large job to fulfill. I know I can do this and I know how to do this. Sally took Aunt Millie's favorite saying and turned it around to help herself: "Cooking is a fine art, and I am a fine artist."

Sally kept reassuring herself with thoughts such as these throughout that whole week. The event went off beautifully. And Sally's menu was a huge success. Needless to say, she received many compliments that night and the satisfaction of quite a few referrals.

More importantly, Sally had learned the importance of dealing with her negative thoughts by giving them her attention, if necessary, and then putting them behind her. Some of our thoughts are just passing through like traffic; others need to be addressed. You will know when a negative thought needs to be dealt with because it will create feelings of anxiety and apprehension in you. It's important to listen to your negative thoughts so that you can better understand whence they come. After all, part of human development involves dealing with situations as they arise in order to understand more about ourselves and grow.

✦ THOUGHT TO THINK ON ✦

You cannot prevent the birds of sorrow from flying over your head, but you can prevent them from building nests in your hair.
—*Persian proverb*

Insights into Negative Thoughts

1. Don't send your negative thoughts away or try to hide from them.
2. Listen to your negative thoughts as they arise. Deal with them so that you might lay a good foundation for your future.
3. Identify the source behind the thought. Could it be a voice from the past?
4. Remember, we learn and grow when we are willing to examine our thinking.

TABULA RASA

Now that you know what to do with negative thoughts and situations, you're ready to wipe the old slate clean and start anew. *Tabula rasa* is a Latin term that means "clean slate." Picture a blank canvas. When you look at the empty space, see the infinite possibilities it holds.

When you think of the blank canvas in this way, there is nothing negative about it. It is up to you to fill that canvas. And remember, this is no time to be skimpy. Paint with a broad brush and vibrant colors.

The blank slate allows you the space to paint your goals. Allow your imagination to flow freely and expand your potential by painting different ways to reach your goals. When you paint your goals and desires on your slate, use all of your senses as your brushes. Don't just paint a visual picture; imagine how it feels, tastes, and sounds. For example, if you are in the catering business and you want to grow, your visual painting might start with having a larger facility and more people helping you. But don't stop there. Imagine the aroma of delicious food cooking in the ovens, feel the bread dough being kneaded, hear the sounds of happy customers praising your culinary skills.

Remember, you are the artist, and only you have the power to change or add to your canvas at any time. Your blank slate is something that you can mentally call upon for a self-motivational boost any time of the day and is a complement to visualization (chapter 5).

✦ THOUGHT TO THINK ON ✦

The future is born in the present.

Insights into Tabula Rasa

1. The blank slate allows you the space to paint your goals.
2. The blank slate is a tool for entrepreneurs to use for self-motivation and inspiration.
3. Remember, *you* are the artist, and you have the power to change your canvas at any time.
4. The blank slate is a convenient way to use your imagination to create the entrepreneurial life you want.
5. Creating a blank slate when you feel the need to wipe out negative thoughts and emotion allows you to get a fresh start.

OPINIONS ARE MANY AND FACTS ARE FEW

When people tell you what you can't and shouldn't do, they are often not telling you the facts but merely stating their opinions. That's all! Just opinions. And sometimes those opinions are of no value to you.

During the third grade I had a wonderful teacher, although it took me close to twenty years to realize it. Miss Daley reigned over our classroom during the days of corporal punishment, or as it was more commonly referred to, paddling.

Miss Daley scared the daylights out of my classmates and me. As strict as she may have been, she taught us the kinds of things that we would use long after the third grade. I remember her teaching us how important it is to understand the difference between facts and opinions. She explained how understanding the distinctions between the two could determine our success or failure in life, and she relied on a simple analogy to demonstrate this: "The fact: It's raining outside. The opinion: It's a bad day."

We must all be able to assess and draw distinctions between facts and opinions when we hear them. We've got to be able to zero in on our own lives and determine, when we hear things about ourselves, whether they're facts or opinions. If you practice distinguishing between the two, then you can eliminate countless potential setbacks. Rely on yourself. Decide whether the information that has come to you is a fact and then act accordingly. Trust and believe in yourself and your own judgment as to what action to take on an opinion.

Kelly's Story

I know a very determined toy-shop owner named Kelly. Kelly is intelligent, energetic, and honest. Her customers and employees adore her, and her store offers the largest selection of stuffed animals and dollhouses in the area. Even though Kelly does quite well, I often wonder how much better she would be doing if she had chosen to build her business around her first love, electronics.

"Because I'm just under five feet tall and weigh 101 pounds,"
Kelly once told me, "I wouldn't be taken seriously in the elec-
tronics business. I know that this is true because several suc-
cessful people have told me so. Because I'm so small, kids and
parents trust me when I make a suggestion. That's why my
store has done so well."

With Kelly's ambition, know-how, and likable personality, I believe
she could have gone far in the electronics business. The electronics
business lost out because of Kelly's decision to sell toys instead of
appliances. After all, who wouldn't want a good, knowledgeable, and
honest salesperson to help them pick out a new stereo or satellite
dish?

Kelly translated others' opinions about her height and weight as
factual information. This kept her from pursuing her real dream. The
most ironic part of Kelly's story is that the people who told her she
wouldn't be taken seriously because of her height and weight are the
same ones who call her whenever they need help with their new tele-
visions or VCRs.

When I started my first business, my father told me that I would
never be able to make enough money to support myself, let alone a
child. He said that I had ruined my life and suggested that I turn my
attention toward finding a husband who would show mercy toward
me and be willing to take care of me and my baby. I realized that he
thought his advice was sound and that he meant well when giving it
to me; I also knew he believed that what he was saying was a fact. Because of Miss Daley, I knew his comments were opinions and nothing more. And because I knew his opinions were only what *he*
believed and not what I knew to be true, I was able to accomplish far
more than he could've ever dreamed for me.

We've all been given this type of guidance before: "You're too shy
to sell anything." "You'll never make it in the dog-eat-dog world of
business." "Why, I know somebody who's already tried that and it
didn't work for them." "I never pictured you as . . ." These are just
some of the kinds of things that people say either overtly or covertly.

Often you'll get more discouragement than encouragement from those around you. One of the ways to rise above such comments is to take them as opinions, not as facts, and know that opinions are many and facts are few.

✦ THOUGHT TO THINK ON ✦

Every opinion is waiting to be changed by a new idea.

Insights into Facts and Opinions

1. Most of the time, advice from other people is based on their opinions, not facts.
2. Notice the difference between facts and opinions when listening to others. Remember, the fact: It's raining outside. The opinion: It's a bad day.
3. Rise above discouraging comments of others by recognizing that most of the time it's their opinion and somewhere in the world somebody has already proved them wrong.

SELF-CONFIDENCE: WHERE ARE YOU WHEN I NEED YOU?

Self-confidence, along with self-esteem, comes and goes. There are times when we feel more confident than others. And there are times when our self-esteem seems to have gone on an extended vacation. However, there are ways of getting both self-esteem and self-confidence back to center stage where they belong.

I've been searching for years for a good definition of self-esteem. Recently, I found one that I like: the ability to be unaffected by other people's opinions.

Self-confidence and self-esteem are built on a series of minisuccesses. As I said earlier, although having large, distant goals may be critical, it is even more important to have some smaller, more immediate goals. They allow you to achieve the small successes that will build the confidence that you need for greater ones. There's an old saying, "Once bitten, twice shy." An example of a "twice shy" person might be a child who is afraid of dogs because he had a bad experience with one. For example, when first meeting the animal, the child, like most children, was curious, though a little afraid, of the dog. Then, as the child moved closer, the dog growled at him. Now the child is twice shy of all dogs. In other words, the child's confidence around the dog, or any dog thereafter, lessened.

But what would have happened if, when the child approached the animal, the dog wagged his tail, gave a friendly bark, or performed an amusing trick? The child would feel confident moving closer to the dog and even petting him. Then, when the child came across another dog, he would most likely feel comfortable with that dog, too. Given his positive experience with the first animal, he would be confident around dogs. He would have achieved a minisuccess that would give him confidence around all dogs. The trick is to remember those minisuccesses that we achieve, no matter how insignificant you may think they are. Look at how Susan worked with minisuccesses:

Susan's Story

Susan always believed that she could sing. From the time she could talk, she was forever putting on musicals for her family and the neighbors using her hairbrush as a pretend microphone and a broom as her microphone stand. Everyone always told her what a lovely voice she had.

Even as an adult, Susan's dream remained constant; it never diminished. So she decided to pursue it. She began to market herself as a singer, for any occasion. Suddenly, those people who had been encouraging her all those years began to voice their misgivings—loud and clear!

"What do you mean, you want to sing? How are you going to do that for a living?"

"Are you crazy? Do you know how many people are out there trying the same thing and have failed?"

"You want to do what? Why don't you just join the church choir, for God's sake!"

These people's opinions certainly weighed heavily on Susan. But she remained determined. She began by putting herself out there. She voluntarily sang at various community events and would receive standing ovations. Each successful engagement gave her a little more confidence. With each step she made toward becoming a professional singer she would mentally recall her standing ovations and praise from her audiences. Finally, she had her own business cards and brochures made and distributed them wherever she went. She made video- and audiotapes of herself at events for anyone interested in seeing a sample of her work.

Eventually, her hard work and determination paid off. Susan began with small opportunities: weddings, community fairs, parades, and so on. With each new success, Susan began to feel better about her decision to fulfill her dream, and those successes paved the way for more opportunities. Susan is beginning to sing on a steady basis and now has to book herself in advance for these events! Her next goal is to have her own compact disc produced. Susan's motto: "One small success at a time."

And her family and friends? Ask any one of them now what they think of Susan and you will most likely hear, "Well, you know, we've been telling Susan ever since she was a baby that she should be singing!"

If you can string together a number of these minisuccesses, making sure to give yourself credit for them, you will gain momentum. You will build confidence and strength, and prepare yourself and your thoughts for much larger successes.

✦ THOUGHT TO THINK ON ✦

Success breeds self-confidence. Self-confidence breeds self-esteem.

Insights into Self-Confidence and Self-Esteem

1. Dwell on your strengths, not your weaknesses.
2. Hear people out, but remember, they are generally giving you their *opinions*.
3. Keep a tally of each success you achieve—*no matter how small*. Keeping a minisuccess journal can give you the fuel that you need for continued success.

CHOICE IS YOURS; CHERISH IT

The decisions and choices we make can determine our entire future. Sometimes we'll find ourselves going against the grain, but we still have to make decisions that will shape our lives. Whatever decision you make, it's *your* choice, not anyone else's. Even deciding not to decide is a choice. Every day, every minute of every hour, we are making choices in our lives. Sometimes the choices are very minor, for example, what to eat for lunch. Sometimes these decisions are major, that is, what to do with my life. Whether the decisions that you make from day to day are minor or major doesn't matter as much as the fact that *you* make them. It's another way to take charge of your life.

Sometimes we find ourselves in situations that seem to offer no way out. Yet it is often after we hit rock bottom that we make our best choices.

During my pregnancy, I believed that I would be able to support

myself and my child through my own business. It didn't take me long
to realize that life can be difficult and the world is filled with people
who want to tell you how to live it. Other people's values and decisions were coming at me from all directions, telling me that I needed
to find a husband, that I should forget the idea of running a business
and go out and find a job, or that I should give up my baby for adoption. What if I had left my choice up to someone else? What if I had
given my baby up for adoption? Where would I be now? I would have
given away my reason for succeeding in my life. But at fifteen I knew
I had to make this major decision of my life and the life of my child,
and certainly, at this stage, I still had days of doubt and fears. I had
only my limited environment, not years of experience and wisdom,
for guidance.

But Grandma, who had years of experience, shared some of her
wisdom with me. She was an avid, twice-a-day Bible reader and encouraged me to do likewise. She often told me that no matter what
problem surfaced in life, the solution could be found somewhere in
the Bible. The problem that I faced at that time was having many
people tell me how ridiculous it would be for me to try to run my
own business. I should stay at home and care for my baby instead.
I knew that I should do the right thing, but what was the right
thing to do? I didn't follow Grandma's prescription—reading the
Bible twice a day—but I did find myself reading it periodically in
search of solutions to my problems. She was right. It didn't take me
long to find solutions in the Bible. The story of Mary and Martha gave
me the inspiration to live a life of my choosing and make my own
decisions.

Mary and Martha

Jesus and his disciples were welcomed into the home of Mary and
Martha, the sisters of Lazarus. The two women busied themselves in
the kitchen, preparing a feast for the men. Mary, overhearing the conversation in the next room, realized that Jesus was imparting wis-

dom. I believe that Mary wanted to lend a closer ear so that she could hear all that he was saying, so she chose to leave her kitchen duties behind and become an eager listener of the wise teachings. Martha became very upset at being left alone to cook and serve, and so she complained to Jesus, "Lord, don't you care that my sister has left me to do the work by myself? Tell her to help me!" Jesus answered, "Martha, Martha, you are worried and upset about many things, but only one thing is needed. Mary has chosen what is better, and it will not be taken away from her." (See Luke 10:38–42.)

Mary had a choice between tradition, in this case kitchen duties, and listening to the wise teachings of Jesus. She chose the latter. My guess is that she felt this would allow her to be empowered by the lessons that were being taught.

Even though my choice was not nearly as dramatic as Mary's, it had a significant impact on me. It was clear to me that it was okay to want something different from, or in addition to, what is usually expected of us. At the time that I read this story, it seemed to me that Martha was content with the status quo. That appeared to be the path that everyone was trying to get me to follow. On the other hand, Mary wanted something different and therefore made a choice that seemed to be nontraditional.

The roles of Mary and Martha are equally important. As my life progressed, I came to realize that there's a time to be Martha and a time to be Mary. In fact, I viewed these women as two sides of one person. We need our Marthas in the world, and we certainly need our Marys. Mary's choice became a big step and a meaningful one for me. Her choice gave me the courage and confirmation that I, too, could choose my direction in life even though it was not the "norm" at that time.

Have the courage to choose your own direction, too. It's a gift. Don't treat decision making as a burden, although, at times, it may seem that way. Cherish your ability to choose for yourself, to choose your own path.

♦ THOUGHT TO THINK ON ♦

There are three things that man must know to survive in this world: what is too much for him, what is too little, and what is just right.

—African proverb

Insights into Choice

1. Make the kinds of decisions that will shape your life.
2. Even deciding not to decide is a decision.
3. Having the courage of our own convictions can help us make wiser choices.

SELF-INQUISITION: WHO AM I?

In conjunction with building minisuccesses, another way to gain confidence is through self-inquisition. Self-inquisition is the ideal way of finding your true self, your talents and skills, and it forces you to stay focused. It requires you to question yourself constantly. If you don't keep questioning your motives and actions, you will not only lose confidence; you will lose focus and, eventually, your customers. Self-inquisition is not just a way to know yourself; it's a way to get to know those around you, for it will give you the habit of questioning your actions, as compared to theirs.

Every day, nearly every hour of every day, you're faced with decisions and challenges, and many require a unique approach. Approach these situations through self-inquisition and consistently ask yourself: What does this mean to me? Where do I want to go? Why? How will I get there? When examining yourself, keep in mind that it's seldom wise to accept your first answer, for it is usually the easy answer. It's the answer that lies at the forefront of our minds, allowing us a chance to lay the blame elsewhere if our lives don't work out as we would like. In order to function in a successful business and develop a full life, we need to know who we are, where we are, and where we are going, which requires getting to the core of our true selves. Rarely will accepting the first answer take us there. Be diligent when digging for answers about yourself and your goals; sometimes it may hurt, but it works. Adopt the habit of self-inquisition and apply it to your business and private life. Whether it's to run your business or deal with family, self-inquisition will help you sort out who you are, and is important for your continued growth and success. The following story about Jeff provides a perfect example of this process at work:

Jeff's Story

When Jeff reflects on the early days of starting his own greenhouse and nursery business, he recalls his "third degree" approach. Each step along the way of his career, he asked himself tough questions to "keep himself on his toes."

Why do I want to start my own nursery? What is it that I truly want to accomplish by doing this? What can I do for my potential customers better than anyone else? To strengthen his self-inquisition, he kept a journal. Every evening, he answered his own questionnaire! He also applied this method of thinking to each customer. Can I furnish my customer with what he wants? If I don't have what my customer needs, how can I go about getting it for her? What would work best for what my customer really wants?

Jeff's third degree was an incredible asset to him *and* his customers. This process constantly reminded him of who he was, where he started from, and where he was headed. And it paid off. His customers love him! They know Jeff will be able to help them with whatever they are looking for; if not, he'll find other resources if he doesn't happen to have what they need. The result of this approach is happy customers and a thriving business. Jeff also uses this technique at home with his family, creating a harmonious atmosphere.

Be inquisitive about yourself. If you don't know how, watch a group of small children; they are the most curious self-inquisitors around. They are able to take something complex and put it into a simple question. Always look for answers, and when you've found them, come up with more questions. This will not only "keep you on your toes"; it will certainly keep you in good stead with your customers, your family, and your friends. Like Jeff, I have found it helpful to keep a journal of the questions that I ask myself. It allows me to delve more deeply into who I am. Find the real you and go beyond the first answer.

✦ THOUGHT TO THINK ON ✦

The questions which one asks oneself begin, at last, to illuminate the world, and become one's key to the experience of others.
—James Baldwin

Insights into Self-Inquisition

1. To know the real you, question yourself regularly.
2. In order to reach deeper levels of your true nature, don't be tempted to always accept your first answer.
3. Keep a journal of questions that relate to improving your business and your life.

A SENSE OF RENEWAL

To cope with the stresses of everyday life and gather the fragmented pieces of ourselves, we all need someplace that we can retreat to that will refuel us and give us a sense of renewal. My sense of renewal comes from sitting in my favorite chair in the living room and looking out the large bay window at the big, old oak tree in my front yard. It has been there for a long time, longer than I have existed. Its roots reach far beyond the confines of my yard. And when I'm gone, that old oak tree will still be standing there. That tree is strong and seems to be impervious to the chaos of the world around it. While contemplating the tree, I realize that even the oak tree has a life cycle. A cycle of positive and negative forces affect that tree. It will bend with the wind, it will lose its leaves, it will grow buds and leaves, its sap will rise and fall. Through all of these changes that tree will continue to stand tall and strong. When I reflect on that oak tree, I feel stronger as a human being: I realize that, like the oak tree, all of life is a rhythmic cycle. Watching the seasons change is like watching our lives. The fall and winter are like a withdrawal of nature into itself, a time of rest and quiet, a declining, so to speak. And then spring and summer come, and we enjoy a fresh sense of renewal and rebirth.

Each of us is subject to the ebb and flow of nature. If you can come to understand, appreciate, and accept this natural, inevitable rhythm of life, you will find your own inner strength. Our bodies have a natural rhythm, as does all life. When we learn to accept and appreciate these rhythms and the strengths and weaknesses that they bring, we can have inner peace, a kind of spiritual awakening that doesn't necessarily have anything to do with God or religion but is an acceptance of certain universal truths about the way life works.

If we don't take the time to renew, we will eventually throw our lives out of balance. What if you don't change or replace the oil in your car? Well, pretty soon it won't drive as well. Ultimately, the engine will stop, and the car won't run at all. By not changing the oil, the engine will burn out, for the car's cycle will have been knocked off kilter. The same thing could happen to you and your business if you don't take the time for renewal, for proper, routine maintenance.

Life works in a rhythmic cycle; it has a push and pull to it. There will be strong days and weak ones, and inherently we know this. But sometimes we get caught up with things in life and forget how it really works. Remembering and understanding the rhythmic cycle will give us a good foundation of inner strength and self-confidence.

Look at a baby—any baby who's learning to walk. He pulls himself up and then falls down. He pulls himself up again, takes a step, and falls down. Over and over he will go through this process, until one day he takes one step, then two, and finally toddles across the room. The baby doesn't know that what he is trying to do is next to impossible. He only *knows* that he can do it and therefore continually works at the process of doing it. It is an inherent "knowing" that is working in the child.

There's something on the inside working for that baby: drive, will, and determination. There's also encouragement on the outside for that baby: *us*. We applaud the baby. We encourage him to take steps even though he risks falling on his face. We say, "You can do it, come on, you can do it." We don't tell the child, "No, you cannot walk on two feet, so give up." However, that same child grows up and hears others echoing: "You can't, you shouldn't, and I wouldn't if I were you." And enough of that can make any individual forget the inherent will, determination, and confidence that it took to stand on two feet in the first place. You have to reclaim that original drive and hold on to it tightly in order to take necessary risks. Reclaiming your inherent strength means remembering to find what refuels you and provides you with a sense of renewal. For me, the oak tree stands tall as a reminder of life's rhythmic flow and helps me to recall my inner strength. For you it may be the change of seasons or observing the habits of wildlife or something else. But whatever it is, find it *today* for a better *tomorrow*.

✦ THOUGHT TO THINK ON ✦

The will to do, the soul to dare.

—*Sir Walter Scott*

Insights into Renewal

1. Reclaiming your inherent strength means remembering to find what refuels you and provides you with a sense of renewal.

2. A daily refueling will keep life in balance.
3. The more we can come to understand and appreciate the inevitable rhythm of life, the more likely we are to find inner strength and peace.

WRAP-UP

As you ponder over becoming a successful entrepreneur, think about how important your thoughts are to your goals in life. Instead of allowing your thoughts to occur randomly, take control of them. When you find your business and your life off balance, try looking at your thinking first. Are your thoughts getting in the way of your success? By looking at the thoughts you choose to think on, you can measure your progress, or lack thereof. Make a commitment for the rest of your life to **live your life consciously.** Remember, if your thoughts are negative, let them go. If they are positive, embrace them and let them fuel you.

During the process of taking charge of your thoughts, think of yourself as an impervious oak tree. Know that no matter how much it rains or how hard the wind blows, you will remain standing tall. Like the baby who is taking his first steps, remember your determination, ambition, and drive. Even when it is your own doubts that knock you down and not outside forces, pick yourself up and walk on. Address any doubts that you may be having and always question what others say to you. **You are what you think.**

REVIEW

Become **aware** of your "thinking thoughts."
Reaffirm your purpose each day.
Practice focusing on your strengths and uniqueness.
Set goals that you can see.
Build your business with what you have at hand.

The **power to control** negative thoughts is in your hands.

Remember, opinions are many; facts are few.

Self-confidence **comes and goes.**

Choices are yours for the making.

Practice self-inquisition.

Live life consciously.

You are what you think!

Chapter 2

OVERCOMING OBSTACLES

✦

In my fourth month of pregnancy I knew I had to figure out how I could make enough money for my baby and me. I had to determine what marketable skills I had. One day, while reading the newspaper, I saw an ad placed by a woman who offered her ironing services to others. I realized that I could iron, too—that was a skill that was in my limited repertoire at the time—so I placed my own ad in the paper.

When women started to show up at my door with baskets filled with their husbands' shirts that needed to be ironed, I knew I was in business. But after a few weeks I realized that I didn't like doing it. Standing in front of a hot ironing board all day was no fun, especially in July, the hottest month of the year. Apparently my lack of enthusiasm for the job was showing, since I started to get complaints from irate customers who said that I was ironing too many wrinkles into the shirts. So I unplugged the iron, and with a girlfriend I started selling fire extinguishers and fire alarms door-to-door. Although this endeavor hardly proved to be a flaming success, it netted enough to pay my doctor bills, buy a few outfits for the baby (who was due in a couple of months), and give my grandmother a little money for her hospitality, since she had been nice enough to allow me to move in with her.

However, as I got closer to my delivery date, it became tougher to climb the steps of each home and even more difficult to run from dogs who lay in wait under porch furniture for anyone or anything that even slightly resembled a salesperson. But what really put out my fire about this venture was finding out, during a front-porch demonstration for a testy husband, that the fire alarms didn't work. No matter how close the man held a flame to one of the alarms, it wouldn't go off. As a result, I learned an early lesson about selling. Know your product.

I retired from that business and, along with two girlfriends, launched an early version of Meals on Wheels—not for elderly shut-ins, as we know it today, but for jitney drivers and gas-station attendants who had money to pay for good home-cooked meals but neither the time nor the desire to prepare them. We solicited lunch orders each day by telephone—fried fish (which we scaled ourselves), chicken, potato salad, green beans, and candied yams, which we cooked in my grandmother's kitchen. We each brought our individual talents to the business: I cooked, one of my friends put the food on plates and covered them with foil, and the other, who had access to her family's car, made deliveries. In the end, the profit margin was small, and smaller still when split three ways. And, like ironing, scaling and frying fish is a tough way to earn a living. Nevertheless, I had earned enough money to support the baby when she came.

Within two months after the birth of my baby girl, I had embarked on my most lucrative venture, the one that taught me the most about the business world. I answered a want ad in a magazine placed by a Bible company in Kansas that was looking for salespeople. Once again, counting on my most mature, confident telephone voice, I called the company.

I was able to convince the sales manager that I had an incredible sales force and could certainly sell fifty family Bibles (at $49.95 each) in thirty days. And I did indeed have an incredible sales force. I was it. Selling fifty Bibles in thirty days was important because the more I ordered and prepaid, the less the wholesale price. I managed to persuade the sales manager to send me the first fifty (at $8.00 each, wholesale, the total due in thirty days). By this time I had realized that in business one encounters one obstacle after another. And for me, a big obstacle was constantly having to figure out how to make money without investing it, especially since I didn't have any. This led me to understanding step two of entrepreneurial success— **OVERCOMING OBSTACLES.**

BEYOND OBSTACLES

One of the most powerful things we can do is to get over, under, or around the obstacles that stand in our way. Each of us will encounter many through the course of our lives. As with every other aspect of our lives, those of us in business have our share of obstacles to deal with. An obstacle can be defined as an obstruction of some sort, something or someone that gets in your way. I once read that an obstacle is what you see when you take your eye off the goal, and to a great extent that is true. But more important is what happens when we come face-to-face with the obstacle. I have learned that by changing the way we see obstacles and how we respond to them, we can disarm them and make them weaker. By weakening them, you can make yourself and your business much stronger.

An example of this is a track-and-field event, hurdles. If you've watched any Olympic track-and-field event you've probably noticed that even the best hurdlers will occasionally knock over a hurdle as they head for the finish line. According to the rules, that's perfectly acceptable. The runner's main focus is the finish line; however, he must encounter each hurdle, deal with it, then get beyond it.

Running hurdles does not involve running around them or clearing each one without ever making contact with it. As a businessperson, you must approach your path to success in the same way a hurdler approaches his race. There will always be obstacles; do not ignore them or expect to overcome them neatly and cleanly every time. It's best to face, and deal with, each obstacle in a way that allows you to exert power over it, thereby allowing you to be in control.

Sometimes it's difficult to recognize obstacles. There are so many little things that can hamper your success, that can hold you back, things that you don't even recognize as problems. We are all products of our experiences, our background, our cultures, our families, and in many cases we also become *victims* of our experiences. Unwittingly, we adopt theories, ideas, and concepts that can become obstacles. For example, if I had known that an inner-city teenage single mother would be perceived as a failure by society, imagine where I'd be today. Probably writing my grocery list while waiting for my check to come. As a young girl, I didn't know what failure was, nor did I think about it. Sometimes obstacles have been preprogrammed into our minds, like the opinions of others. Remember the difference between a fact and an opinion from chapter 1? Opinions are many, and facts are few. Understanding this can serve as a catalyst to guide us in our businesses. Our obstacles, like others' opinions, only have as much power as we give them.

Sometimes we are our own worst enemy. For instance, there's a type of thinking that psychologists call "catastrophic thinking." It occurs when you see everything, every circumstance, in the worst possible light. For example, you're driving to a meeting with a potential client and encounter a traffic accident that causes a major delay. You start to think, If I can't get past this traffic jam, I'm going to be late. If I'm late, the client will think I'm incompetent, and I won't get the contract for his business. If I don't get this contract, I may not find another one. If I don't get another contract, I might lost my house. If I lose my house, I'll be out on the street. This may sound extreme, but many people engage in this type of thinking every day. An entrepreneur with a new business may think after the first couple of months of low sales, I may have to close my business and give up everything I've worked so hard for, without thinking through what strategies might work to increase business. And there are other ways that we can sabotage ourselves. Many times I have heard people say, "I would be able to make a go of it . . . except . . . except . . . except my friend doesn't think it's a good idea, except the bank won't give me a loan," or, "except I have five children and a wife at home who are very nervous about this." We all go through this kind of mental and verbal sabotage. The truth of the matter is that we have control over the answers. What I have learned to do is to take things one at a time.

If traffic is backed up, I think of an alternate route rather than waste energy being frustrated or upset or thinking about all of the bad things that could happen to me because I am delayed. If I find myself stuck in traffic, I sit back and relax or listen to an inspirational or self-help tape. Or perhaps I'll use the time to meditate (but only while my car and I are sitting still!).

One Sunday morning I needed to get to my office while a marathon was taking place. When I encountered a blocked-off street, I thought about the local transit authority. Surely they would have alternate routes planned in preparation for the marathon. I used my car phone and called the local bus company to find out what route they were using from the area where I was to where I needed to go. And I took that route. I could have viewed the closed streets as obstacles, but I didn't. By not seeing the closed streets as potential obstacles keeping me from my destination but merely a temporary inconvenience, I was able to get to work as planned.

We all face obstacles in business, whether it's an obvious one, such as a roadblock due to a marathon, or a not-so-obvious one, such as a friend's "advice" or a loan officer's *opinion*. It's important to realize that our perception of the obstacle will dictate how much of an impact it will have on our lives. Realize that it's perfectly okay if your friend doesn't agree with your plans and that most people in business can't get money from the bank when they need it. I didn't know at the start of my business that banks even *went* into business with people (thank goodness I didn't know), so my business grew as a result of profits. Turn your excuses into positive motivators. For example, having children and a spouse at home seems like all the more reason to be in your own business and to want to live a balanced life. Wipe the slate clean and then write on that slate what you want. Take a look at where you are and then think about where you want to be; then try to spot all of those existing roadblocks that have been created by others and adopted by you. Rise above those obstacles so that you can move ahead toward *your* goals—not where somebody else THINKS you should be. Think and be where YOU want to be. Walt, for example, knew exactly what he wanted and where he was going:

Walt's Story

What's the last thing you spent forty dollars on? Perhaps you bought a new pair of shoes, a couple of compact discs, or treated a friend to dinner. Walt, an entrepreneur, took forty dollars and started a company. While staying with his uncle, he used the small garage in the back of his uncle's house as a makeshift workshop. It was there that he constructed his first camera to produce animated comic films. Once he could afford to, he invested a little money, along with his brother, and rented a small office located in a real-estate building down the street. Soon after, the brothers moved their business next door to a much bigger space. The name of their company was the Disney Brothers Studio.

The point is, Disney started from what most people would view as "nothing." Luckily, Walt knew better. He knew he had talent, skills, and creativity. Of course, his life, like every entrepreneur's, was filled with naysayers. In fact, when Snow White *premiered, W. C. Fields, a giant in Hollywood at the time, was quoted as saying that no one would sit through a movie-length cartoon, especially one in color. He felt the film would hurt people's eyes.*

Walt had taken out a second mortgage on his house to produce Snow White. *He must've had doubts about his venture already. Then a major actor publicly denounced his efforts. Walt hadn't allowed his doubts to stop him from making* Snow White, *and it was a huge success. Today the Disney company stays true to his goal of producing at least one animated feature every year while reaping millions of dollars in profits.*

Sometimes you don't notice that a habit, stereotypes or superstitions, or the expectations of others and how we interpret them can become obstacles. Perhaps the biggest obstacle is the lack of knowledge, particularly if you don't know how to find needed information. Do a self-examination and ask yourself, What are my obstacles?

✦ THOUGHT TO THINK ON ✦

My life has been filled with terrible misfortunes—most of which never happened.

—Mark Twain

Insights into Beyond Obstacles

1. Keep in mind that when you are constantly looking at the obstacles that may or may not occur, *you are no longer seeing your goal.*

2. Rise above your obstacles by changing the way you respond to them. Disarm them and take away their power, thereby making them weaker.

3. Deal with an obstacle by turning it into a positive motivator. For example, instead of believing I don't have the money to do this, believe I have to do this because I don't have money.

4. Recognize that your obstacles may merely be mirages created by you due to your experiences: habits, stereotypes, superstition, the expectations of others, or lack of knowledge.

GUILT AS AN OBSTACLE

One universal obstacle is guilt. It is placed in your path by people who are attempting to manipulate you. Inevitably you will encounter such people in both your business and your personal life.

Sanford and Son, an old TV show starring Redd Foxx, relied heavily on guilt for comedic purposes. Every week, Foxx's character, Fred Sanford, manipulated his son, Lamont, into doing something that he wanted done. Often he did this by convincing Lamont that behaving contrary to his wishes would cause the "big one," a fatal heart attack. Lamont would fall for this week after week.

Perhaps Lamont found it easier to meet the demands of his father, often doing things he didn't want to do, than to live with the guilt that *he* had caused Fred's death. The way to counter this manipulation and to remove the "hurdle" of guilt from your track to success is to trust your common sense. Think of Fred and Lamont. Lamont failed to see that he had no power to stop the "big one" from striking Fred.

How can you tell when somebody's putting a guilt trip on you? You know because of how you feel. When you find yourself doing something you really don't feel good about or don't want to do, pause and ask yourself, Why am I doing this? Will this help me advance to my goal, or have I permitted someone or something to introduce an obstacle in my path?

I have two terrific granddaughters whom I love very much; however, I don't always feel like baby-sitting them. Sure enough, when it's not convenient for me, my daughter appears and gives me at least a dozen reasons why I should rearrange my schedule to watch the girls. She might say: "But you're going to miss their development" (never mind that they live a block away) or, pathetically, "Okay, I'll just stay home again." Whenever she tries to use that guilt tactic, I'm very comfortable saying, "Well, hire a baby-sitter. I have something else to do this time." I know that I love my daughter and granddaughters and that being firm about not changing my schedule doesn't change those feelings one bit. It allows me to avoid being manipulated. When you find yourself being manipulated into doing or agreeing to do something when you had other plans, chances are someone's trying to make you feel guilty. Spend quality time with your family and friends but make sure you save some quality time for yourself, too. However, keep in mind that at times it may be important to sacrifice yourself for others. Sometimes I say yes to watching my granddaughters, even though I had something else planned, and it turns out to be a wonderful and enjoyable experience. The difference between my attitude and Lamont's is that he acceded to Fred's whims *every* time.

The best way to avoid guilt is by giving the best of yourself. When you have dedicated yourself to your work, family, and society and given the best you have to offer, you don't have to feel guilty when people ask you to do things that you can't do or are not interested in doing. If you treat others with respect, honesty, and integrity, then you've done all that you can and have no reason to feel guilty for refusing them. When you have given your all and are satisfied that you have done your best, there should be no room in your life for being made to feel guilty. It is thus important to know yourself, trust your instincts, and above all, recognize your responsibility to yourself.

✦ THOUGHT TO THINK ON ✦

It takes guts to avoid guilt trips. Don't let them scare you.

Insights into Guilt as an Obstacle

1. Guilt is an obstacle placed in your path by others in an attempt to manipulate you.
2. When you find yourself doing something you don't want to do, ask yourself whether you are doing it out of guilt.
3. It's okay to go along with another's wishes sometimes, as long as you recognize that you are not just giving in because you're feeling guilty.
4. If you've given your best, there should be no room for guilt in your life.

INTERDEPENDENCE

Every entrepreneur wants and needs people in their lives and in their businesses but also requires his or her own space. I call this push and pull between the need for others and for solitude interdependence.

German philosopher Arthur Schopenhauer used an analogy about porcupines to illustrate the concept of interdependence. He explained that the animals, when trying to make it through the winter, huddle together for warmth, but then their sharp quills prick each other, and they pull back. However, when they pull back, they get cold. The porcupines will continue to huddle together again, only to be pricked once more by one another. Inevitably, they will be forced to pull back again.

The porcupines are constantly trying to adjust their closeness as well as their distance to keep from freezing to death. At the same time, they attempt to position themselves strategically to avoid being pricked by other porcupines. Like the porcupine, we need to learn to constantly adjust our closeness to others—whether family, colleagues, or customers.

What I'm talking about is finding the balance between space and closeness, dependence and independence, that will allow us to be with others and ourselves more effectively and comfortably. This can happen when entrepreneurs come together with other entrepreneurs. For example, I recently took part in a symposium for entrepreneurs that was designed to allow us to interact with each other, exchanging thoughts and ideas so that we could maximize our potential without losing control over our projects.

We divided into groups of five. Each person gave a fifteen-minute presentation to her group, five minutes discussing her accomplishments of the previous years and five minutes spelling out her goals and objectives for the future. The final five minutes were spent talking about the obstacles that she would have to overcome to reach her goals. After our fifteen-minute presentations, each of the other four entrepreneurs in our group offered their feedback, sharing their thoughts, ideas, and in some cases contacts that could be made to help overcome any roadblocks in reaching our goals. Each entrepreneur, in turn, then gave his or her presentation to the four, and again thoughts and ideas were shared.

At the end of the session, a wealth of knowledge had been tapped, and a host of new ideas had been exchanged. Thus, like the porcupines, we had come together to share our "heat." It was up to each of us, however, to act on or discard those items that we had shared. In other words, we had to decide how much of the advice we had been given we wanted to use—exactly how dependent on the group we wanted to be.

This is an example of interdependence. Those ideas that we felt were useful could be acted upon; we could discard those that were not. In this way, we were able to avail ourselves of the help of others without compromising our goals and the path that we felt was the correct one to follow in attempting to fulfill them. As an entrepreneur, we must constantly attempt to form these types of interdependent partnerships and relationships. In this way, we can obtain fresh ideas and feedback that will strengthen our own decision-making processes.

Remember to take time out to be able to distinguish and analyze all of the "quills" that you encounter. Being interdependent allows you to stay close enough for warmth and protection from the support and comfort of others, but far enough away to avoid being hurt or overly influenced.

✦ THOUGHT TO THINK ON ✦

Entrepreneurs create and develop each other.

Insights into Interdependence

1. Call three or four entrepreneurs to get together a couple times a years for sharing information, ideas, and resources to increase each one's success.
2. Interdependence is the middle ground between independence and dependence.
3. Interdependent relationships give you the benefit of having control over your business while at the same time allowing you to open up to new strategies and ideas of other businesspeople.

FEAR OF FAILURE

Besides guilt and manipulation, there are two other obstacles that are very common in business and in life: the fear of failure and the fear of success. How do you eliminate your fears? By not eliminating them at all.

The fear of failure is easy to understand. There is nothing as paralyzing as thoughts of failure. Why start the marathon if you're afraid you're not going to finish the race? Why start the business if you're afraid you're going to lose all your money? Or write the book if you're afraid it's going to be awful? Experience shows that if you *fear* you will *fail*, because the thing that you feared would happen often does.

Acknowledge the fear, face it, even talk to yourself about it. Get to know it. It is through this process that you will neutralize the fear and weaken, though not necessarily eliminate, it. When questioning your fear, determine whether it is "productive." Some fears are important to our success. The fear that keeps you from jumping off a bridge is a good one. The fear that drives us to produce excellent work because we might lose a client can be healthy for a young entrepreneur. But you need to recognize the difference between fears that are real versus those that are perceived. Let's take a look at how Fred handled his fear of failure:

Fred's Story

Fred had a nice little accounting business going for himself. He had a sizable list of customers and was living quite comfortably as a single man, running his own ship. He was even able to throw in a few extra goodies for himself at the end of his fiscal year. But then problems began to occur, though at first nobody could figure out why. But Fred was beginning to notice a pattern.

Things were going better than they ever had; business was good, as was life in general. His work wasn't quite the same. Accounting errors were beginning to add up over a period of time, and customers were beginning to complain about the quality of his work. Neither had ever happened before.

Fred began taking inventory. There was nothing wrong from a business standpoint. However, it was when he began looking inward that Fred noticed that things were not so stable. He had reached a crossroads in both his life and his business. Just recently engaged, he had begun planning for the future. It was time to take his business to the next level to prepare himself for his and his new wife's future. While Fred always knew he wanted to expand, it wasn't until that thought actually became a reality that Fred discovered just how frightened he was. Keeping his business on a smaller scale, just to meet his needs, had always been quite simple. Fred was in a comfortable, secure rut. Deciding to change that left him with many questions. How would he go about doing it? A future family put things in a different perspective; he would need to provide for somebody other than himself. Competition had increased also. All of these factors were leaving Fred feeling a bit insecure about himself and his business. There were times when he felt overwhelmed by uncertainty and had doubts about expanding. After all, he was doing fine all these years. Why risk a good thing?

Fred was setting himself up for disaster. His fear of failure was clouding the goals he had set for himself at the start of his entrepreneurship. Fred needed to take a good look at his fears and confront them before they defeated him. In time, he was able to do this. Gradually, he got his business back on track. He decided to sell his services to new entrepreneurs and comfortably grew his accounting company by more than 50 percent. Fred is now married and with a new baby on the way. Whenever he looks back, he realizes that his fear of failure could have impeded his success.

"I never knew how big my fear of failing was until I was able to confront it and work through it. But believe me, there were times when I could feel myself nearing a panic attack at the thought of it all."

The "big picture" can be intimidating. A good rule of thumb is to avoid constantly looking hard at that picture. Spend more time looking at the smaller picture in front of you each day and gradually (as with successes) prepare yourself for the big ones. By taking small steps, you will reach your larger goals. In Fred's case, this meant recognizing that his fears about expanding his business were getting in the way of running it all. He focused on getting his work back up to the level his clients had come to expect. Having achieved that, he was able to start planning the business's expansion.

✦ THOUGHT TO THINK ON ✦

Great things are done more through courage than wisdom.

Insights into Looking at Our Fear of Failure

1. Do you notice when things are not going so well in your business? If this is a pattern, could it be your fear of failure creeping in?
2. Are you afraid of failing? Try to discern *why.*
3. Remember to set goals that are within your reach. Don't dwell on the "big picture."

FEAR OF SUCCESS

While waiting in line at a local deli, I overheard two men exchanging greetings. "Hey, Joe, how's it goin'?" one said. Joe responded with a foreboding "Man, things are so great, I'm scared." That statement says a lot about the fear of success. It may be even more difficult to understand than the fear of failure, but it's just as relevant. It seems hard to believe; who on earth would be afraid of succeeding? Plenty of people. And they are so afraid of success that they become a "failure attacher," attracting everything and everybody that will inhibit their success. There are a number of reasons why. Some people feel that even the slightest bit of progress means that they will lose the acceptance and approval of friends and family. How often have we heard offhand comments and criticism when we are trying to make headway, for example, something as simple as reaching a desired weight. I observed a woman constantly criticize her son's weight while he worked hard, through diet and exercise, to drop fifteen pounds. She nagged him about how thin he was getting, asking him if he was sick. If he wasn't, she would say that he sure looked sick to her. He soon drifted back into his old life of fast-food eating and no exercise. He could have ignored his mother's badgering, but he wouldn't have pleased her.

Another example of how the fear of success can entrap us is the "riding high in April, shot down in May" syndrome—the idea that if you aim high, your fall is certain. One day, shortly after I bought a new car, a woman that I know saw me drive into the garage at work and stopped by my office to comment on how nice the car was. She then advised me that I should consider either taking the bus to work or buying an older used car just to drive to and from work. When I inquired into the logic behind her comment, she said that most people would stop using my company if they thought that I could afford such luxuries. I didn't listen to her, but these are the kinds of comments that can plant seeds in our minds that create a fear of success. And when that fear takes root in our minds, we will create, or be drawn to, every possible situation that will impede our progress. Let's take a look at Katherine:

Katherine's Story

Katherine had a very successful beauty boutique. The women who made up her clientele had been established customers since she had opened the shop three years earlier. They enjoyed the atmosphere and the pampering and constantly reminded Katherine that her line of products was the best ever. Katherine would say on many occasions that her success was too good to be true. Moreover, Katherine's best friend, Nan, would agree with her.

Katherine had managed to save a good deal of money due to the success of her business. One day, Nan stopped by the boutique to borrow several thousand dollars from Katherine, explaining that she had an extreme emergency and would pay her back over a period of three months. Katherine explained to Nan that she needed her money to buy beauty products for her business. Nan told Katherine not to count too much on her business because success is short-lived. After all, she told her, "your friends are there when everybody else has forsaken you and you're down and out." Plus, she said, "Your clients are no different; they are just people who will start to get too demanding when they think that they are making you rich and quickly move on to someone else, leaving you looking like a fool for having believed in them."

Katherine loaned Nan the money. As it turned out, Katherine got a large order for her products and needed her money to buy supplies. Eight months had passed, and Nan was either ducking her or making up excuses about the delay in the repayment. Katherine was unable to fill her order. She soon found herself unable to keep up with the demands of her customers, which was unusual for her, for she rarely made a customer wait for anything. Her profits slowly began to diminish, and her bills started to pile up.

Katherine called me, and we met for lunch. She talked about how her business was in a mess and that it was all because of her friend Nan. I asked Katherine if she thought that she might have set herself up because she was afraid of success in her business. Though she thought my idea was crazy, she admitted that she knew that Nan was unemployed and had not worked in the three years they had been friends. Nan had been unable to borrow money from banks due to bad credit. Finally, she had loaned Nan money in the past that she had not been repaid. Katherine admitted that these were warning signs that

Nan was a bad risk. She also thought back to other friends with whom she had had the same experiences. After Katherine listened to herself sharing her story with me and answered a few questions, she agreed that her successful business had frightened her and that deep down she had known that Nan couldn't, and wouldn't, ever pay her back.

Katherine's boutique suffered that year. Shortly after our meeting, Katherine joined an entrepreneur's association, which allowed her to meet successful entrepreneurs with whom she could share success stories. She rebuilt her ailing business and became the accommodating beauty-boutique owner that her customers had grown accustomed to. She also got rid of Nan as her friend.

There are many people who are so afraid of succeeding that in order to shield themselves from success, they search for people who will slow them down or place obstacles in their path, someone who will drain their energy and give them an excuse to fail. There are many who think that if you're making money, if you're doing well in your life and business, something awful is on the horizon. Some people stand around waiting for "bad things" to happen; still others get impatient waiting and go looking for it. Because of the old mentality that "money is the root of all evil," most people expect something awful to happen to them because they are doing so well in their business. Whether we are getting these messages from others or from our own inner voice, it is important to pay attention to how we think. We have to examine and reexamine ourselves so that we can recognize these obstacles, deal with them, and discard them.

One thing to keep in mind if you feel you might be afraid of succeeding is that it is extremely critical to keep an account of your every accomplishment, no matter how big or how small. Write them down in a place where you can visibly see them when you need to. That way, you can plainly see with your own eyes that you *are* successful, that you have *already* succeeded.

Because both the fear of failure and the fear of success have caused so many entrepreneurs problems, we are going to take a closer look at both. Fear is an emotion caused by a real or imagined sense of an impending negative event. Fear in itself is not negative, especially for entrepreneurs. Fear of failure can be a very positive tool for anyone launching a new project. As long it doesn't immobilize you, making it impossible for you to follow the plan that you have devised to achieve your goals, it can keep you constantly alert to the pitfalls awaiting you. Just as it is good advice to "know your enemy," it is also good advice to know your obstacles before they can impede your progress.

It is therefore crucial that you pay attention to your voice of intuition that warns and cautions you as you move along your chosen path. I once heard someone say that the "entrepreneurial road to success is always under construction," and I agree that there *are* many roadblocks along the way. Let your fear of failure alert you to them and use that fear as a tool to prepare you to meet and defeat them. Never let it stop you from trying; use it to your benefit by intelligently dealing with problems before they become insurmountable obstacles to your success. As long as you use your fear of failure to work for you and not against you, it can then be viewed as another tool in your storehouse that can be useful in making decisions that are in your best interest.

Fear of success, on the other hand, is a more destructive process. It causes you to make decisions that are against your better interests. When you fear success, you let irrational thinking cause you to make choices that hurt your chances of reaching your goals. To feel that achieving victories in your effort to be successful must be evidence of impending bad luck is self-defeating behavior that will doom you to eventual failure. Instead of facing challenges and opportunities with confidence and positive thoughts, you look at these opportunities with fear and apprehension. Consequently, you become incapable of moving forward and achieving your dreams. You let irrational fear hold you back and destroy both you and your business.

Fear of success can also be caused by external factors and individuals. Some people have your best interest at heart but suffer from the same irrational idea that success must breed failure. Thus, they influence you to be afraid of obtaining your goals and enjoying your accomplishments. Some, for their own reasons—envy or jealousy—try to plant seeds of doubt that cause you to question yourself and make decisions that will eventually lead to failure. In order to be a successful entrepreneur, you must see fear of success for what it is: a destructive process that must be avoided.

Fear of success and fear of failure are therefore different in their impact on your life and your business. One, fear of failure, can be a useful tool, while the other, fear of success, can only be a destructive obstacle. You cannot, however, afford to ignore either. You must be aware of all those forces around you that filter into your decision-making processes. Rid yourself of those that are destructive to your reaching your goals and harness those that can help you achieve them. It is the successful entrepreneur that can distinguish between the positive and the negative and always move forward with realistic caution and strong confidence.

✦ THOUGHT TO THINK ON ✦

It's a wonderful feeling to succeed. And you're allowed to feel it!

Insights into What to Do When Fear Sets In
1. Get rid of people who make you feel fearful of your success.
2. Cross-examine the fear; analyze it to find out if it's fear of failure or success. If it's fear of failure, see it as a signal to tighten up any loose ends that might be obstacles to your success. But if it's fear of success, take it as a warning to check to see where your fears originated.
3. Invite people into your circle who want to see you make progress and are willing to help you achieve it.

CRITICISM

Another obstacle you will encounter is criticism from people around you. Your family will tell you what you're doing wrong. Your friends will warn you that you could fail, and they will relate stories of others who failed at endeavors similar to your own. Understand that these people are speaking from their own fears of success or failure; it's their problem, not yours. There will be many obstacles that you will face along the way in life and business. Obstacles, or challenges, as they are sometimes called, can't be avoided. What we can do to make our path to success a little less rocky is to make certain that the obstacle or situation that we face belongs to us and not to someone else.

If you're an Olympic hurdler, you don't leave your running lane to jump over someone else's hurdles. So why spend your time jumping over hurdles that stem from the fears of other people? Give yourself the gift of disregarding the fear-based criticism of those around you. Even though your "critics" feel that they are only looking out for your best interest, never countenance or absorb what they're saying. My grandmother used to say, "Child, that just went in one ear and right out the other." Don't let the fears of others even enter your first ear. Learn to feel this kind of criticism coming and create a space between yourself and the critic. When I am approached by someone ready to criticize me or offer unwanted opinions, I visualize (in my mind's eye) a bright, shining star on the face of the person talking. As a consequence, the person thinks that I am looking at him or her and listening intently. The truth is, because I have concentrated my attention on the star, my eyes only see a star, and my ears hear nothing. I have found this to be a peaceful way of giving myself the space that I need during these types of encounters, especially since it is generally the people who love you the most (family, friends, etc.) who are the most critical. This is a learned skill, but once it is mastered, it becomes part of you. Once the boundaries are set between you and your critics, you will immediately be able to sense when somebody's about to say, "You can't, you shouldn't, I wouldn't if I were you," and then you can enter your space.

Keep in mind that there are times when you need to listen to criticism. It is especially important when that criticism is coming from someone who means to empower and encourage you. That's the person you need to listen to, the person who has been to the places that you're trying to get to and has already done the things you want to do. We'll talk more about that type of person in chapter 4, "Building a Dynamic Support System." Meanwhile, let's see how Joe handles his critics:

JOE'S STORY

Joe is an entrepreneur with three successful hardware stores. When asked what he attributes his success to, Joe answers, "My critics!"

"When I started out with my first store, I left a pretty decent job where I had been working for nearly ten years. All of a sudden I had instant critics!"

Everyone felt the need to interfere in Joe's life with their opinions and criticisms.

"What are you doing this for; you already have a good job?" and "Hardware stores are a dime a dozen; you're leaving a good job and the security that comes with it" were common criticisms.

Ironically, this fueled Joe's fire even more. At first, he couldn't tell to whom he was proving a point, himself or his critics!

Joe says, laughing, "I felt this extra drive to succeed every time somebody criticized me."

You can bet that when Joe made the decision to expand to another store, he heard a second volley of critical remarks. "Isn't one enough, why risk a good thing?"

All in all, Joe did open another hardware store, and to the amazement of his critics he eventually opened a third one!

"My advice to entrepreneurs is to always prove 'em wrong. Take the good criticism and disregard the rest."

So you see, it's important to realize that criticism is just another version of someone else's *opinions*. Everybody has them. And they won't be too shy about sharing them with you whenever you are entertaining the thought of straying from the beaten path or doing things differently from what others feel is correct. Ultimately, what you do with your critic and their criticism is your choice. Just make certain that it enhances your growth and development. Sometimes, like Marsha, you may welcome your critics' opinions:

Marsha's Story

Well into the second year of owning a flower and gift shop, Marsha was struggling. Her sales revenue was all right, but she found she was still having problems making enough profit by the end of a month to pay all of her expenses, and her debts were mounting. She was puzzled by this, because she was precise with her purchases and carried only the most expensive lines of collectible gifts in her shop. The customers seemed satisfied, and she typically had a steady stream of customers.

One day, a woman who frequently visited her shop for certain items approached her and struck up a casual conversation. Soon Marsha discovered that this woman was also a business owner. Naturally, the discussion led to business, and Marsha asked her if she'd ever gone through a similar situation during the growth of her business.

The woman seemed hesitant but replied, "When I first started my business, I tried to keep my purchases very basic. I found quality items that I needed at reasonable prices. While I always wanted to have the best in my shop, I simply couldn't do it for those first few years."

The woman paused for a moment because she didn't want to offend Marsha. Nor did she want her to think that she was being pushy. Still, she thought, Marsha had asked for her opinion. She continued in a gentle manner: "You have some really beautiful things here. But the items are too pricey. Even though you have a lot of people coming in, most are just looking and not buying. Maybe you could cut back on some of the expensive items. The important thing is to get the traffic in the store and build customer loyalty and trust. Once that happens, they will spend more on expensive items. Display more items that are of quality but reasonable in price. That way, you can still meet your business expenses at the end of the month, make a profit for yourself, and enjoy the benefit of many satisfied customers."

Marsha didn't feel offended at all. In fact, she took the lady's advice to heart and slowly began to make the changes that she had suggested. Over time, she was able to pay her bills and still satisfy her customers' needs. After adhering to this plan for a while, Marsha was able to get her business to a more comfortable place, which, in turn, allowed her to gradually upscale.

What is pivotal in Marsha's story is that she listened to this bit of criticism and decided to follow it. Marsha could have very well thought to herself after the other business owner had left, I can't believe the very *nerve* of that woman, telling me she thinks that my gift items are too pricey and how I should run my business! She could have thrown that advice right out the window, along with her already escalated debt. But she didn't. She absorbed that piece of information and was able to use it to her advantage.

So you see, as in Marsha's case, learning the difference between negative and positive criticism can be a major key to helping you in your business endeavor. In time, you will know which critics to listen to and which to ignore.

✦ THOUGHT TO THINK ON ✦

The difference between negative criticism and positive criticism is the way it leaves you feeling inside. Judge all criticism from your internal thermometer.

Insights into Dealing with Criticism

1. Regard criticism for what it is—others' opinions.
2. Bear in mind that people generally think that their criticism is in your best interest.
3. Remember that what you do with criticism is *your* choice.
4. Learn to recognize helpful criticism and use it.

A WORD FROM THE WISE

Sometimes wisdom comes from where you least expect it. So it's important to keep your eyes open and recognize it when it shows itself. The universe will present you with wisdom when you least expect it, so be prepared. Wisdom can be unpredictable, so don't make any presumptions or you could miss out.

Sometime ago, there was a very large account I wanted, but I was very doubtful that I could land it because I was competing with much larger travel companies. One day I was talking with Mildred, an older woman who used to come into the travel agency often. She had never been in business herself and would often say that she didn't know a thing about it. Yet she was always eager to talk to me about how my business was doing. And I did indeed enjoy talking with her. On this particular day, Mildred asked me how things were going. I shared with her that business was fine; however, I was bidding on a corporate account that I had my doubts about being able to get. As far as I was concerned, my chat with Mildred was all just conversation in passing, with no particular motive or idea in mind other than responding to her question "How's business?" Mildred said, very softly and yet with a smile, "What are you worried about? God hasn't failed you yet, has he?" She waited patiently for my answer. I replied quietly, "No." And she added, "So what makes you think he's gonna fail you now?"

The truth of her statement was a reality check for me. I was jolted into realizing that I had temporarily lost faith. Faith in my skills, in my abilities, and in my conviction that divine influence was always working with me. My attitude changed instantly. And do you know what? I landed that contract.

For a moment I had forgotten, and Mildred's wise and timely statement brought me back to reality. I have heard her words of wisdom echoing in my mind many times since that day. But I also knew that if I didn't get whatever it was I wanted, then the way was being paved for something better.

Wisdom comes in many different forms, sometimes from the most unexpected places. Stay open to receive wisdom when it comes. It can serve you well for the rest of your life. Oh, and by the way, that two-year contract that I landed back then turned into a twenty-three-year contract!

✦ THOUGHT TO THINK ON ✦

Once wisdom touches you, it refuses to be ignored. It will echo inside you over and over, in your dreams and in your waking thoughts.

Insights into Seeking Wisdom

1. Don't assume wisdom comes only in the form of Gypsies, wizards, and lightning bolts. Real wisdom usually comes in the most unexpected packages.
2. Typically when something profound has been passed on to you, you will *feel* it. It will strike a very familiar chord in you.
3. Once you've been blessed with a bit of wisdom, don't forget it or let it go!
4. Remember how you felt when someone said something to you that you needed to hear at that time; share it with someone else. Maybe they will be fortunate enough to "get it," too.

SOCRATIC METHOD

I can't emphasize enough the importance of self-inquisition. Although we discussed self-inquisition in chapter 1, we are now ready to delve more deeply into it.

The great philosopher Socrates was famous for his "know thyself" approach to life. He spent his life talking to himself, asking questions, and seeking better and more truthful answers. He and the Socratic philosophers who came after him believed that the meaning of life involved the ability of man to know himself.

A proven method for getting to know more about yourself is to write things down, and not necessarily in a journal or diary; you don't need anything that formal. However, keeping a journal will give you something to review and note the progress that you've made. If a fear or an obstacle enters your path, write about it. Write down the question and then write the answer. Write: "What is it about this situation that bothers me?" and then your first answer. But remember that the first answer is rarely the right one. Probe for the deeper meaning of your situation. If someone upsets you, write about it. And then write why you think you were hurt or upset. If your first answer is something like "Because I just don't like that person," then ask, "Why?" Continue the Socratic method until you get to the root of why you are upset. Writing your fears on paper will help you face them better. As long as they are tucked away inside, it's easy to bury them or hide from them. Bring them out into the open by writing them down. Facing problems and dealing with them will remove them.

The Socratic approach and writing things down will allow you to confront fears and obstacles and to search for truth. Fear is usually not based on any truth at all. There are exceptions, of course. For example, if you are on a life raft and you see a row of shark fins approaching, your fear is probably based in reality. The fins have sharks attached to them, and they may be looking to have you for dinner. However, the kinds of fears you will encounter in business are not as obvious or realistic in their nature. Don't be afraid that you'll screw up your sales pitch. You are not a reckless idiot. You are a well-prepared, reasonable, and responsible person. The fear of failure is absolutely not based on fact. Self-talk, or the Socratic method, will help you find the truth.

Remember that obstacles such as guilt, doubt, and fear have no inherent power over you or your mission. Only *you* give your obstacles power. If you approach them correctly, you will have power over them. Once you realize that you are stronger than your obstacles, then you can encounter each one of them, deal with them, and then move on toward your goal.

✦ THOUGHT TO THINK ON ✦

Knowing others is wisdom. Knowing the self is enlightenment.
—Lao-tzu

Insights into the Socratic Method

1. Like Socrates, you should continually be asking yourself questions and looking for better and more truthful answers.
2. To get to know yourself better, write things down. Write: "What is it about this situation that bothers me?" and then your answer. Continue to write the questions and answers until you find the root of your problem.
3. Recognize that obstacles, such as fear, have no more power over you than you allow them.

KEEP YOUR MOUTH SHUT

Confidentiality is a concept utilized by military strategists. Pursuing your endeavors in secret, thereby avoiding or bypassing possible opposition, is another way to avoid obstacles.

Tom's Story

Tom's family and all his friends and neighbors knew that he loved to putter in the makeshift woodworking shop in his garage, but no one knew about his dream. For years, Tom honed his skills and squirreled away hundreds of items, knowing that someday he would start his own business. The one co-worker he had told about his dream thought he was crazy to even think about giving up his secure job as a software engineer. Looking for sympathy, Tom told his wife about his co-worker's opinion. Tom's wife just said, "Honey, I think you should think twice about this." After that, Tom never told another soul. He just started going to weekend craft fairs to test his products, telling his wife he was working overtime. Tom learned the value of keeping his mouth shut. He sold out every item each time he presented his crafts at the fairs. Now he owns a thriving woodworking business and has expanded from his line of craft-fair toys to custom cabinetmaking and his garage shop to a factory employing thirty-seven people.

In my life, many of the missions that I start are in secret, carried out behind the scenes. This prevents people from surrounding my intended project with negative energy; they never get the chance because they don't know what's going on. Keeping your intentions secret is an effective way to avoid naysayers or critics. You don't need to have people talk you out of a situation or give you their seal of approval. Too often, when you share information with people before beginning your project, you're secretly looking for someone to say, "Ahhh, this is a good idea," or, "Uhmmm, I don't think that's gonna work." Unless the people whom you are consulting have succeeded in getting to where you want to be, consider carrying out your endeavors quietly and secretly.

✦ **THOUGHT TO THINK ON** ✦

It is in silence and darkness that seeds grow.

Insights into Keeping Your Mouth Shut

1. By carrying out your endeavors in secret, you can avoid possible opposition.
2. If no one knows about your project, you can keep it from becoming surrounded by negative energy.
3. Take advice from those who can help you. With all others, keep your mouth shut!

OPPORTUNITIES IN OBSTACLES

There are times when an obstacle can be an opportunity. Again, it's all a matter of perspective and approach. All of us have heard people we know or have read about complain about being laid off for one reason or another. Most often it's a corporate position that has been eliminated. Usually these people are despondent when talking about a layoff, yet often it is an opportunity in disguise for them.

Recently a good friend of mine called me in a depressed state. As she put it, she had given seventeen years of her life to a local corporation as the best public-relations person the corporation had ever known. According to her, she was thanked for seventeen years of loyal and dedicated service with a farewell lunch hosted by her supervisor—and a pink slip. And I couldn't help but ask her what, exactly, bothered her about this situation. She indignantly answered, "What bothers me is that I don't have a job."

"But you have talent, you have skill," I countered. "Maybe you ought to look at this problem as an opportunity to really use your skill for yourself and the hundreds of entrepreneurs who need you."

After much coaxing and coaching by me, she started her own public-relations business, directed at helping small businesses become more visible in their communities. And her business has become quite successful. More often than not, hidden behind a problem *is* an opportunity.

For example, it appeared that with a child and no job, I had a problem as a young woman. Was it a problem? Maybe. But I turned it into an opportunity.

Sometimes we have to take a look at the things we encounter and ask ourselves, Is this really a problem, or is this a chance for me to do something else with my life? But don't get the impression that it is anything other than what it is: a problem. Problems generally have to be dealt with; they need solutions. But you have to determine when you have a problem that can be changed into a chance to expand or one that requires a different solution. The difference between a problem and an opportunity is how you look at it. It can be a problem to be out of work and have no skills, talents, and resources; an opportunity exists if you're out of work and you have skills and talents and resources. Put them to work for you. And if your skills or talents can benefit others, you can be certain that if handled properly they will prove profitable to you. So if you have skills and talents, maybe the downsizing your company is going through will become a bright opportunity for you, the talented person. Even the "problem" for the unskilled person gives him or her the opportunity to develop a skill. That's the solution.

Not all problems are opportunities, and not all problems have to be dealt with. Some problems have to solve themselves, like a bad haircut. Through our self-analysis, knowing who we are, and the utilization of common sense and intuition, we can determine just what action we need to take.

✦ **THOUGHT TO THINK ON** ✦

Bear in mind that often, during the most difficult times, a brand-new opportunity lies in wait.

Insights into Opportunities in Obstacles

1. Determine if the situation is an obstacle or a hidden opportunity. Or is it a problem that only time will cure?
2. Review your skills, talents, and resources when addressing problems and obstacles and use them to help you.
3. Approach problems with the attitude that overcoming them is an exciting challenge.

RISKS

Many entrepreneurs fail because they believe that business involves obstacles, risks, and problems; so does getting out of bed every morning. It's just as difficult to maneuver and operate in life as it is in business. All too often we have been led to believe that there is something happening in the business world that is mysterious; there isn't. The business aspect of your life is the economic aspect that you use to drive your existence. You are the driver, and you entered your own business to give yourself more of an opportunity to be in that driver's seat. There's nothing mystical about it. There's as much risk in running your business as there is in going downstairs to your kitchen and plugging in the coffeepot. Doing either can bring you enjoyment or create problems.

Many people who are in the driver's seat already or are trying to get into that driver's seat sit there with an "Oh my Lord, what have I done," self-defeating attitude. When you improve your economic situation, then you are at the helm of your own life. You're not being controlled by someone else's ideas. So is there a risk? Some. But I can think of a few things that make being your own boss seem simple. What bigger risks do parents encounter than trying to raise a youngster and present them to the world in fifteen or twenty years, praying every step of the way that they haven't raised a monster? Developing a business is nowhere near as difficult as parenting a child. Yet millions of people will have two, three, four, or even five children and think nothing of the responsibilities inherent in parenting. And many of them will cry the blues about their fears of being entrepreneurs. There's very little, if anything, that will happen to you as an entrepreneur that you can't handle with a little know-how and common sense.

The real difference between the entrepreneur and the nonentrepreneur is who's in the economic driver's seat. Either you're responsible for the money that drives your life, or someone else is. If you're already in business, you're in better control. Take advantage of every opportunity you have to get more control over your life.

Mike's Story

Mike's successful building-contracting business came in the disguise of an unforeseen tragedy. While coming home from work twenty years ago, Mike was dumbstruck to find that a terrible storm had uprooted a huge tree in his yard and that it had fallen through the entire second and first floors of his home!

"I was in shock," he said, "and to make matters worse, I had just canceled my homeowner's policy because we were in the process of selling our house to buy another."

Needless to say, the sale of Mike's house was off. Now what could he do? That's where his skills came in. Mike's father had been a carpenter all his life, and Mike had grown up learning a skill from one of the best. "So," he decided, "I would rebuild my home with my own hands."

Well, that particular project took about two years to complete, and soon afterward Mike was inundated with telephone calls from people asking who his contractor was.

All of a sudden a lightbulb in Mike's head went off. He began his own building-contracting business. Business was very slow at first, but Mike wanted it that way until he was certain that this was what he really wanted. But now, twenty years later, Mike's business is booming. The calls have never stopped coming in. Mike laughs and comments, "Who would have thought that out of something terrible could come something I love so much!"

Like Mike, you must search for the opportunities that life has to offer, even if those opportunities present themselves in the guise of an obstacle or a problem. Sometimes opportunity knocks; at other times you have to pursue it. One thing you don't want to happen is for opportunity to come in on a boat when you're standing around at the airport waiting for it. You have to be WHERE it is. Learn to access your situations and figure out how you can turn things around to work for you. Opportunity comes in many different forms and shows up in many different places, but you want to be in the right place, at the right time, when it appears. If necessary, refer to the Socratic method to help you recognize those opportunities.

✦ THOUGHT TO THINK ON ✦

Keep in mind that very few problems are insurmountable. The way we view them and how we deal with them determine our personal successes or failures.

Insights into Risks

1. Risks are inherent in everything we do, both personally and professionally.
2. If you can raise a family, you can grow a business; there are risks in both.
3. When you think that being an entrepreneur is risky, think of how being at the helm of your own life and not under the control of others are well worth it.
4. How you view risk shapes the course your business and personal life will take. If you can minimize your fear of taking risks, you can take those that are required for personal growth and success in business.

ANGER

Feeling yourself getting angry with someone or something can also become an obstacle if you needlessly expend a lot of energy. When you effectively use your energy to solve a problem and bring about a positive change, you are making positive use of your anger. For example, think of the story of Harriet Tubman. According to history, when she learned by hearsay that her slaveholder was planning to sell her to someone else, she decided to run away. Now we can all say that she ran because she was afraid. I would agree. Except that she kept returning to rescue other slaves and lead them to freedom, creating what became known as the Underground Railroad. My guess is that fear could have been the reason that she ran. However, I believe that her awareness of, and reflection on, the many years of indignities, degradation, and human suffering that she and others had endured during slavery made her angry. And that anger evoked the kind of courage that she needed to risk her life by returning to the South many times to help slaves escape from bondage into freedom.

When your anger prohibits you from producing a positive change, then it becomes self-destructive. This often happens when anger is not vented at the right time and directed at the right people.

For example, say that you're driving down the road and you spot a motorist ahead of you waiting to enter your lane. There are no cars in front of you, but the driver continues to wait. Just as you approach the motorist, he pulls out in front of you, causing you to slam on your brakes as he speeds on. You're now frazzled and upset, but you can't vent your anger on that driver because he's long gone. You arrive at your business still upset by the experience and take it out on a staff person who has made a minor error in his work. On the other hand, if you discover that a staff person is hiding important work in a desk drawer instead of doing it, then anger can be used to communicate how serious the problem is and allow you to begin finding a solution.

Everyone gets angry; it's a normal human emotion. But you need to recognize when your anger isn't productive. Control your anger; don't let it control you. The Greek philosopher Aristotle said that anyone can become angry; that's easy. But he also said that to be angry with the right person to the right degree at the right time for the right purpose and in the right way is not so easy or within everyone's grasp. Consider Aristotle's suggestion and learn to stop and decide which category your anger is in. Is it positive anger that will produce human benefit? Or is it negative anger that produces high blood pressure, ulcers, and hurt feelings that will inevitably create roadblocks between you and your goal?

✦ THOUGHT TO THINK ON ✦

Often when you get to the root of anger, you will find fear.

Insights into What to Do with Anger

1. Recognize it and allow it to help you grow.
2. Don't ignore it or it will come back at you with a vengeance.
3. Decide if it's healthy anger or destructive anger that you are experiencing.
4. DEFUSE IT! Discover what works for you and practice, practice, practice.
5. Remember, being angry is not always a problem. It's what you *do* with it that may be a problem.

THE JUNK DRAWER

Cindy, a young woman who worked at my travel company, sometimes had a problem completing the paperwork needed to refund an airline ticket. At times, she dealt with it by sticking the paperwork in her desk drawer, hoping it would disappear. Inevitably, when two or three weeks later it would resurface, she would be in very serious trouble with both her clients and me.

"Cindy," I questioned, "when you put that airline ticket in your drawer, what did you think would happen to it? Did you believe that it would take care of itself?" Cindy admitted that she knew it wouldn't and that she planned to take care of it later but had forgotten where she had placed the problem ticket. And that was not hard to do, because the drawer that she put the ticket in was overflowing with all sorts of useless papers and paraphernalia. Cindy was often teased by her coworkers about the drawer, referring to it as her "junk drawer." The truth is, by putting the ticket in the drawer, Cindy had simply chosen not to face the problem.

When a problem arises, it requires a solution, whether today or in six months. Normally, the longer it takes for you to solve the problem, the more destructive it becomes. So when problems present themselves, you want immediate solutions. The sooner the better so that you can have the freedom and flexibility to move on without dragging all that excess baggage along with you. Don't shove your problems into a drawer and try to forget about them; they won't let you forget.

Another example of the problems that the accumulation of junk and clutter causes in both your life and your business can be illustrated by the following story:

Phil and Dennis

Phil and Dennis had opened their own photography studio after having worked as freelancers for many years. Lifelong friends and professional acquaintances, the two partners could not have been more different in how they approached their business.

While Dennis was meticulous in his record keeping and in the completion of his assignments, Phil was the opposite. Dennis was constantly trying to bring some order to the studio and especially the darkroom, which they shared. Phil had the habit of leaving negatives and proofs wherever they happened to end up after he had developed them, along with empty soda cans and pizza boxes. There were piles of photographs litter-

ing every inch of space, and it took a major cleaning effort on Dennis's part just to be able to complete his work.

Although the business had been open for only two years, it was obvious to Dennis that it was stagnating. They were both excellent photographers, skilled in both the technical and the artistic aspects of the business, but they had few repeat customers or referrals from previous clients.

It was after Dennis received a complaint from an irate customer that wedding pictures promised by a certain date had not been delivered that he took a long, hard look at the way the business was operating.

The constant clutter was taking a toll on their ability to fulfill their obligations. Technically challenging photo shoots were being postponed because Phil had misplaced the work order, and even those that were completed were being misplaced in the clutter. Dennis realized that for them to succeed, they would have to get things under control.

Convincing Phil of this was more difficult. Dennis tried everything, from talking to Phil about the problem to unsuccessfully trying to clean up the clutter himself. Finally, Dennis told Phil that he couldn't take it anymore and thought that the best thing to do was end the partnership. This struck a chord with Phil; he could now see that his clutter was about to end a long friendship and their business. Phil agreed to clean up the clutter. Together they attacked the problem, and their business became organized and efficient. Deadlines are now met, and problems are no long hidden under junk and clutter. Their company began to grow, and instead of complaints, they began receiving awards and praise for their photography.

Phil told me that keeping junk and clutter out of the studio is the hardest thing that he has ever done, but the thought of losing clients and your best friend is worse, so he makes an effort to maintain order.

There are many people, like Cindy with a junk drawer and Phil with his clutter, in both their homes and their businesses. This kind of disorder prohibits your business from growing.

Our surroundings are a reflection of who we are. When we know ourselves, we know our entire environment. If you do indeed have a junk drawer or an office filled with clutter, you may want to do an evaluation of it. Think about it as stuff that weighs you down and serves no useful purpose and consider how many years it's been accumulating. Ask yourself if it has any value and is worth keeping.

When checking out that junk drawer or the disarray, take a moment and check the mental clutter that may be accumulating in your thoughts, and clear it away. It's actually quite easy to spot; it prevents clear thinking and serves no useful purpose.

✦   THOUGHT TO THINK ON   ✦

Understand that until you effectively deal with your problems, they will always be in your "junk drawer." They will always come back until you clean them out.

Insights into the Junk Drawer

1. Problems seldom just disappear.
2. The sooner you solve the problem, the less time it has to grow.
3. Solving a problem is like removing excess baggage.

WRAP-UP

We've talked about identifying obstacles, what they are and what they look like. You've seen the importance of facing problems squarely and promptly and how to differentiate them from opportunities. We've discussed guilt and how it affects us. We've talked about the two important fears, the fear of failure and the fear of success, and how each can have a major impact on our success in life. We've talked about people who are critical of us and ways of applying the Socratic method, about opportunities and the importance of being in the driver's seat of our own economic engines. Obstacles are those things you see when you take your eye off your goals. Therefore, keep a close watch on your goals. You'll be able to see short-term goals more clearly and reach them sooner than you will the long-term goals that you really can't see. Each time you overcome an obstacle and reach a goal, you will have a minisuccess on which to build. In turn, each success will deepen your self-confidence, enhance your self-esteem, sharpen your inner voice, and prepare you to confront your next obstacle and jump the next hurdle.

REVIEW

Remember, an obstacle takes your eye off the goal.

Ask yourself if the obstacle in question is yours or somebody else's.

Recognize guilt. If it doesn't belong to you, give it back!

Don't **become** a victim to any kind of fear.

Recognize and **keep track** of each step toward progress— even the small ones.

Accept positive criticism if you *seek* it; reject the negative. Don't give it your space.

Keep alert for wisdom in all forms.

An obstacle can be an **opportunity.**

Clean out your mental junk drawer.

Chapter 3

ESTABLISHING COMMUNICATION

✦

I had successfully completed my first step: The regional manager of
the Bible company truly believed that I and "my dynamic sales force"
were ready to take the Bible-selling business by storm, and indeed I
was. When the shipment of the good books arrived, I set off with a
supply of them and my baby in her buggy to go door-to-door and convince the people in Pittsburgh's inner-city community of Homewood
that they needed a family Bible that cost more than many of them
earned in a week. I remember my pitch well. "If you don't need it
now, you'll need it later," I told each prospect. I instituted a time-
payment plan: $9.95 down and $5 a week for eight weeks. I sold the
first fifty in two weeks. I also learned the meaning of the word *ex-
haustion*. With a second shipment en route, I decided that there had
to be a better way of marketing the Bible, and I had to find it.

While listening to the radio one day, I heard an advertisement that
caught my attention and thought, Now there's an idea. I'll advertise
the Bibles over the radio. I called the station's advertising department and was shocked when told of the high cost of advertising. But
the greatest surprise came when I was told that they didn't guarantee
sales. My young sixteen-year-old mind couldn't make sense out of
this kind of operation. I spent a half hour on the phone with a radio-
station ad salesperson trying to explain to him that his station should
only be paid if they sold the Bibles. He didn't get it. I pursued another
angle.

Through a friend who was employed as a disc jockey at a local radio station I secured a list of stations throughout the country that aired religious programs. I drafted a cover letter and a simple agreement (patterned from one I found in a book at the public library). With help from another friend, who could type, I produced copies of the letter and agreement and sent them off. The letter pointed out the benefits of offering something special to the listeners of their gospel and religious programming. But what really sold them was the part about how profitable the deal would be for the station. The agreement stated that the radio station would agree to sell the Bibles over the air during their gospel programming at $49.95 each; listeners were to send $24.95 to the station, along with their names and addresses on three-by-five cards. The station would keep the initial $24.95 as their payment for making the offer and send me the card. I, in turn, used the card as a mailing label and shipped the Bible C.O.D. Upon delivery, the post office relayed the C.O.D. payments of $25.00 per Bible to my P.O. box. More than two dozen radio stations responded immediately, and my days of door-to-door selling, standing over hot irons, and frying fish were gone forever.

In order to market the Bibles successfully, I had to find a way to communicate the benefits of owning one to my potential customers. I didn't have the money to pay for radio advertisements, so I had to reach my market creatively through other forms of communication. I had to learn what these forms were and how they worked. This brought me to the third step of entrepreneurial success: **ESTABLISHING COMMUNICATION.**

WHAT IS COMMUNICATION?

Any form of sending or receiving messages is communication. Whether you are marketing or selling your products and services, creating a public-relations plan for yourself, or trying to get the kids to behave, you are communicating. Communication is the most important skill we use in life. As entrepreneurs, it is the lifeline of our businesses. It is a skill we use from the time we get out of bed in the morning until we fall asleep at night. How effectively we communicate will make all the difference in our success, not just as entrepreneurs but in the many other roles we play. Good communication skills will take you further in life faster than you could ever dream possible. The subject of communication is so large that entire books are written about just one or two of its specific elements.

This book looks at communication from the standpoint of the entrepreneur's business and personal development. First we'll discuss marketing and positioning our businesses and then move into the kind of communicating that we do with ourselves that will enhance our self-image and position us for worldly success. Finally, with the two previous elements in place, we will see how we can interact with others to guarantee our success.

As you can see from my Bible-selling venture, practicing good communication allowed me to take another step in the right direction of successful entrepreneurship. When I entered the business world, I did not use the typical business words, such as marketing, public relations, and strategic plans. I didn't know these words at the time, but I *did* know that if I communicated to the right people in the right way, I would make progress. It was that simple. And a little simplicity can go a long way. To demonstrate this philosophy, let's take a quick look back at the elements of my Bible-selling days.

First, I had to make certain I had something to offer people that was salable, so I looked for the *right product or service.* Then I had to sort out who the people were that would buy my product, *the right people.* Next, I had to figure out a way to *let the people know* that the product was in the marketplace, to *get the product to the people.* In the language of business this is called marketing and sales; at the time I started, I called it *the obvious.* Then I had to make certain that all of the folks who worked to help me get the product distributed received fair and good benefits. Finally, since I had no experience or money, I had to learn how to do all of this creatively.

Communication, or being able to effectively market your product or service and yourself, is critical to your business growth.

✦ THOUGHT TO THINK ON ✦

Effective communication will not only enhance the image of yourself to others, it will enhance your self-image.

Insights into Communication

1. Communication is the most important skill we use in life.
2. How effectively we communicate will make all the difference in our success.
3. Communicate your enterprise to the right people in the right way and watch your business grow.

THE RIGHT PRODUCT OR SERVICE

You know you have the right product or service when you can say, "I use it myself, and it's great." Remember the man I was selling the fire alarm to (in chapter 1) and how he demonstrated to me that it didn't work? You can't imagine how embarrassed I felt. I remember how excited I was the day the five alarms arrived at my door. I grabbed them and ran out the door to make money. It never occurred to me to test the product and make sure it worked. Thank goodness for the customer who did and for another valuable lesson learned. Choosing the right business means finding something you believe in. It will be much easier to achieve success if your business reflects your high values and standards. It was no more excusable for me at age fifteen to sell a bad product than it would be for someone at age fifty.

Entrepreneurs must know exactly what they are selling. Our responsibilities as entrepreneurs are not only to our families and ourselves but also to society. And consumers expect us to present them with safe, effective, and affordable merchandise that WORKS. The amount of profit earned should not be more important than the qual-

ity of the product or service presented to the public. Although to-
bacco companies know now, if they didn't all along, that their products are harmful, they continue to mislead the public, especially
young people, by marketing smoking as a cool and glamorous thing
to do. Now they are beginning to see their profits decline and their li-
ability increase.

As business owners, we also have to keep up with the rapidly
changing environment and the changing needs of people. Keep this
in mind when assessing the right product or service. Make sure that
whatever your business offers, it should have staying power and
adaptability.

An example of how we can adapt our businesses to the changing
conditions of society can be seen in the alterations and adjustments
I made in the travel agency so that it could stay around for a while. In
the beginning of chapter 4 you will read how I got started. But for
now let's fast-forward a bit and take a look:

My Story

*During my first two years in the travel business I successfully
chartered buses and sold seats to individuals for one-day and
weekend tours. But when competitors—clubs, churches, and
other organizations—started doing the same thing with larger
numbers of people, it soon became difficult for me to find forty
people to fill each bus. In order to keep my business alive, I had
to make a change in whom I was selling my travel services to.
On any given Friday evening I would ride by some of the local
organization headquarters and see as many as thirty buses
being loaded with members and friends going on a weekend
trip. I realized that it might be better for me to join this system
than to try to beat it. So I contacted each organization and sold
them on the idea that I could provide them with one-stop shopping. Rather than continuing to do the research for their out-
ings themselves, I told them I could do all the legwork for them
and save them time and money by calling hotels and sight-*

seeing facilities and securing charter buses for them. They agreed, and I became the travel consultant for churches, clubs, and other organizations. It worked out well. It was a convenience for them and income for me. Up to this point, the business worked well from my home; the only office equipment I had was a telephone and a typewriter. However, during this time, home-based businesses were not popular; in fact, they were frowned upon. So in order to meet my need to remain in business and keep my customers happy, I employed a young man as a messenger; he delivered travel documents to my customers' homes and offices and picked up payments. My clients were impressed with this service, and I conveniently continued to run my company from my home without interference.

I had no idea how long the arrangement with the organizations would last, so I started thinking ahead. In order to get my feet wet for bigger and better things, I started designing air-travel packages. My company was small compared to the travel companies that had been around awhile and smaller yet when compared to travel giants like American Express Travel agencies. So I kept my travel packages geared to special-interest groups, such as senior citizens, the hearing-impaired, and high school educational tours. I made lists of the different types of group interests and then researched to see if a travel service was being provided to that market. If not, I would provide the service. The 1970s and early 1980s brought about more growth. By now my business needed commercial space to meet the demands of its clientele. The travel service that I provided was equal to any travel company around, but the time had come when I had to look more like those larger companies, and so the mid-seventies found me moving into a commercial space. Once I found one, I needed the ability to generate an airline ticket that wasn't handwritten so that I would appear as professional as the giants. I found the answer in a teleticketing machine, which I leased.

During the economic recession of the mid-seventies, many

individual travelers had put their vacations on hold. I still had to keep my company going, though. Having made enough money to get real computers, I traded in the teleticketing machine and installed airline computer terminals in the office. I was now ready to tap into the corporate community. I landed contracts with the likes of Westinghouse, Sears, and Pepsi Cola. While still providing for individual vacation needs, the travel agency did exceptionally well with corporations. Then corporate downsizing started, and I immediately felt the pinch. I therefore started moving the company toward the conference and convention business.

Having the flexibility to change and good communication skills made it possible for me to stay one step ahead in business. An entrepreneur has a dual responsibility: to provide satisfactory service to your clientele while taking care of your own needs. I had to be a forward thinker, plan accordingly, and communicate my plans effectively. Are you considering your customers' needs or your own when making business decisions? Are your decisions propelling you toward the future or keeping you in the same place? Are you opening your business at 10:00 A.M. because all the other stores open at this time when in reality your customers need you at 7:00 A.M.?

I once met a man who owned a coffeehouse that opened at 10:00 A.M. because it was a convenient time for him. He claimed that all the other stores around his opened at that time. His company never managed to make a profit. And rarely did he experience a break-even month. Eventually he sold the coffeehouse to a person who he said was "some fool who thinks that he could make money selling breakfast beverages." Five years later, the man who bought the company has a successful business because he opens at 6:00 A.M., in time to catch commuters en route to work. The early opening was also an inconvenient time for the new owner, but he endured the inconvenience until he had made enough money to hire someone to open the store.

Asking yourself where you and your business are going and how you will get there are tough questions, but they can be easily answered if you are true to yourself and your customers. For example, you don't need me to tell you not to get into the typewriter business right now. Sell the kind of service or product that you need and would buy. Listen to your customers or your prospective customers and they will tell you and show you what they want. I once read somewhere that people don't know what they want. And this may be true. But people certainly know what they *don't want*. They don't want complications! They don't want confusion! And they don't want inconvenience!

Be an innovator. Innovators don't pay attention to the competition; they pay attention to the customer. If you focus too much attention on the competition, you will see the same old things and miss the customer sitting right in front of you who's telling you things like "I want an easier way to get the information I need" or "I want a faster way to get information to my customers" or "Wouldn't it be great if my business travel could be hassle-free." Or even, "I don't have $49.95 for a Bible right now, but I could give you a small down payment and $5.00 a week." If you focus on your customer, you will know what product or service to sell *and* how to sell it. And, most importantly, be open and willing to change.

Ada, a woman I met at one of my seminars, had a background as an accounting clerk in a large corporation. She believed that the life of an accountant was the most stressful. And it was proved to her when she had to leave her accounting position because of stress-related health problems. Ada decided to go into her own business. She recalled memories of vendors making irate phone calls and sending nasty letters to the accounts-payable department in search of long-overdue payments on invoices they had submitted. The invoices weren't paid because the employee who engaged the vendor was not sending the proper paperwork through the correct channels, resulting in serious delays in reaching the accounting department. Ada remembers this as an "unnerving" condition to work under. For her own business she developed a problem-solving workshop based on that aspect of her experience, but she was having difficulty deciding how to sell her program and to whom. Although she had sent a brochure to all the major corporations in town, nobody was buying a seat at her workshops, and she couldn't understand why.

The overall message of her workshop concerned getting co-workers to work together effectively by sensitizing them to the problems of the different departments they had to deal with. The first question I asked her was if she thought she was selling something the corporate community wanted. And second, whom within the corporation was she targeting? She hadn't considered who her target audience might be. Together we came up with a plan to identify her target market, in this case the accounting departments, and to get them to buy her program.

The plan that we mapped out was based on her experience and knowledge of how staffers in other departments within a corporation could work efficiently and relieve unnecessary tension with the accounting department. Ada started off marketing to accounting departments in large companies and has recently included the accounting departments in law firms. She now has a very profitable business.

✦ THOUGHT TO THINK ON ✦

A business that makes nothing but money is a poor kind of business.

—Henry Ford

Insights into the Right Product or Service

1. Finding the right business means finding a product or service that you are comfortable providing and which people need.
2. Your business reflects *you!*
3. Profit should never be more important than the quality of your service or product.
4. Be open and willing to change.

THE RIGHT PEOPLE

What would you think if you were watching Saturday-morning cartoons with your kids and suddenly the commercial shouting out of the television was Anheuser-Busch proclaiming: "This Bud's for you"? Or you're browsing through your favorite health-and-fitness magazine and find a full-page ad in color from the folks at Batesville displaying the latest in caskets? After regaining your composure, you would realize they had not considered who their real customers are. However, these are not concerns that we need to have because these companies know *who* their customers are and *where* they are.

It's a good idea to know your target market before you start investing money in advertising or wasting time selling. Start by asking, What does my customer look like? Do your own market research. By knowing in advance who your customers are, you'll save time and money by avoiding marketing to people who aren't interested in your product or service.

A consultant I know asked me to critique a brochure she had created. It was a beautiful brochure with lots of details about her and plenty of pictures. I could tell she had spent a fortune on it. She mailed out twenty-five hundred copies to people she thought were her target market and didn't get a single client despite her efforts. She just couldn't understand it. When she called me, I told her the truth. The brochure was stunning, but it didn't say anything about how her clients would benefit by buying her services.

Originally, I targeted my Bible sales to my neighbors. It took me two weeks of twelve-hour days and miles of walking, pushing a baby buggy, to sell fifty Bibles. I quickly realized that I had to find a place where people who wanted Bibles congregated. I believed that church-goers already owned Bibles, so I knew that the churches wouldn't be the best place to target. But people who listened to a gospel-music program on the radio might need a family Bible.

Usually, the solution to finding the right people requires research, asking questions, and remaining aware of your surroundings. Should you decide to skip the research, then you will learn from the loss of energy, time, and money. It's that simple! I sold more Bibles in the first three days on the radio than I had sold in two weeks while going door-to-door. And what helped me to that end was two weeks of sore feet from pounding the pavement, backaches from hauling heavy Bibles, and a cranky baby who didn't like the door-to-door sales business.

Celeste, another entrepreneur I know, sends information about her small-business-development services to all her friends who are already established in business. We can't use her services. She should be marketing to new entrepreneurs, and if she took time to research the market, she would know who and where the people are who would benefit from her services. In fact, several local newspapers list new entrepreneurs in Celeste's area and what services they need each week. In addition, she could use the business branch of the library to help her reach her target markets.

The best approach to conducting your own market research to help you identify your customers starts with designing a questionnaire as a guide for yourself. The first questions to ask are: Who are the people who can benefit from my product or service? Who is this product for? How is it going to benefit them? In other words, quite often you can find the customer through the product. Then just ask yourself questions about your customers and gear the questions to your product or service. The answers will give you a profile of your target market.

Develop a profile of your potential buyers. Here's a list to get you started:

Who is going to need this product or service and why?
How will it benefit them?
Where do they live?
Where do they work?
What do they do in their spare time?
Do they have children?
How old are they?
Are they male or female?

What do they watch on TV or listen to on the radio?
How much money do they make?

Once you do the research, then it's easy to see who and where your customers are. Be careful not to miss the obvious. Market your infant toys to expectant mothers, of course, but don't forget the grandmas and the grandpas, especially first-time grandparents.

In the process of answering all the questions about your customers, you will discover a lot about how to reach them. Now you will know what your customers look like, where they live, and how they live. YOU will know how the product will benefit them; then it will be up to you to convey that information to THEM. And if your product or service will enhance their life, then you should hurry as quickly as possible to get it to the customer and be sure you let them know how it will benefit them.

✦ THOUGHT TO THINK ON ✦

If you know your product well enough, you'll know who your customer is.

Insights into the Right People

1. Know who your target market is before you spend a dime.
2. Finding your target market requires research, asking questions, and remaining aware.
3. Let your product or service lead you to the target market.

SALES: THAT SPECIAL FEELING

Sales is the step that happens after you have successfully found your market. It is a process of communication that begins with presenting yourself. People must first feel comfortable with you before they can process anything that you may have to offer. This holds true in your business and your personal life. What makes anyone comfortable with you depends on how special or important you make them feel.

Many years ago I went to a sales seminar, and the first thing the instructor said was "You don't sell the steak; you sell the sizzle." He never explained what he meant, but I took it to mean that you sell the benefits of a thing, not the thing itself. For me, the most important, the first, thing to know is the buyer. What if my customer is a vegetarian? Steak or sizzle, I won't make the sale. Let's take a look at an experience that I had with a friend:

Steak or Sizzle

I love the Internet! The amount of information I can obtain by touching a key on my keyboard has been incredibly valuable and timesaving for me. It's a tremendous resource. So I convinced a friend of mine who has her own business to get a computer—and quick. She agreed, and together we went shopping for one.

The first salesman went on and on about RAM, megabytes, gigabytes, CD-ROMs, disc-operating systems, and hard drives. In trying to sell us the "steak," he drove us right out of the store. At the next store, the salesman talked about speed, printer resolution, color, stereo sound, and lots of other "sizzle." My friends eyes glazed over in confusion. I almost couldn't get her to go into the next store.

The third salesman started by asking my friend some simple questions about herself and her business. Then he pointed out how the computer could help her accomplish what she had said she wanted to do. He also showed her how the Internet could be beneficial to her. He made some suggestions concerning the features of the computer that she could use to her advantage. My friend bought a computer from him that day. It wasn't the steak or the sizzle that made all the difference; it was the salesman's approach. He took the time to pinpoint her needs. He paid attention to her and made her feel special. And he showed her how his product could be of great benefit to both her business and family.

Just remember that people want enhancement and improvement. They want products that make their lives easier, that improve the quality of their work and make them feel good about themselves. When people look at your product, they want to know how it can help them. It's human nature.

✦ THOUGHT TO THINK ON ✦

Man doesn't live by bread alone. He needs buttering up once in a while.

—Robert H. Henry

Insights into That Special Feeling
1. Successful sales begin with presenting yourself.
2. Make people feel special and they will be comfortable with you.
3. People want enhancement and improvement. Communicate how your product or service will help them, and they will buy it.

THE RIGHT TREATMENT

Success is not a one-man show. It can't be achieved without the help and support of everyone you come into contact with. The support can come from anyone—a friend who steers you in the right direction, the vendors and suppliers who deliver goods and services to you for distribution, or the people you hire to provide the goods and services to the buyer. Sometimes all it takes is kindness.

In the film *As Good as It Gets*, the character Simon, a painter, tries to find the right pose for his model and suggests that the model just move around the room doing nothing in particular while Simon carefully observes his movements. The model becomes frustrated and annoyed with the lack of direction and asks Simon, "Why are you staring at me? What do you want from me?" Simon's response is "If you stare at a person long enough, you will start to see the human in them." Simon was looking for that pose where the model was just "being" and not doing. It is a good idea for entrepreneurs not to stare but to look for the humanness in people, especially those who are working with us.

One day a man called my travel company with a problem that he had encountered with the airlines. He had booked a flight from Pittsburgh, Pennsylvania, to Aspen, Colorado, with a connecting flight in Denver. The airline of origin had a schedule change that would cause him to miss the flight in Denver. His research found that there was a flight that would connect perfectly to his new schedule. However, the airline told him that the flight had been sold out. The man later told me that he had talked to everybody, from the supervisor of reservations to the vice president of customer service, to try to get a seat. All had explained to him that his only option was to stay overnight in Denver and catch the first flight out the following day. As a rule, the man always made his own travel arrangements and didn't see the need to use a travel agency. But since he was desperate and not making progress on his own, a friend of his referred him to me.

I told him that although I would see what I could do for him, I couldn't promise anything. I picked up the phone and called the airline's reservation department. My call was answered by a grumpy voice identifying herself as Alice. With all of the kindness and consideration that I could muster in my voice, I opened the conversation with "Hi, Alice, this is Gladys from Edmunds Travel. How are you?"

"What do you need?" Alice said abruptly.

"I can hear that you're busy," I said empathetically, "so I'll be brief. You see, I have an urgent situation, and I need your professionalism and expertise to help me through it."

"What seems to be the problem, Gladys? Perhaps I *can* help." When she spoke this time, her voice was much softer.

Somehow Alice was able to find a seat for my passenger. What made Alice change so quickly and agree that perhaps she *could* help me? First, I had identified her as a professional and as an expert; next, and more importantly, I let Alice know I needed her. When you make people feel needed, you make them feel special, and subsequently they will go out of their way to help you. This is only one reason why how you present yourself is so important. Unless you learn to sell yourself successfully to someone and convince them to have confidence, faith, and trust in you, your product or service, no matter how good, won't matter.

The reason I was able to get what I needed from Alice was because I treated her with respect. It sounds like a trite, worn-out expression, but it still holds true today, and it always will: Mind your manners when you're dealing with people. INVEST THE TIME TO FIND WHAT IS HUMAN IN EACH PERSON YOU ENCOUNTER. Think about it, and just as your mother always said, "Treat others as you would like to be treated." Remember, without your customers you are nowhere in your business. If you're like most people, when you go into a department store, how the clerks respond and behave will dictate much of your spending. Keep this in mind as you move toward your goals. Present yourself to people in such a way that they want to help you. If a person can really "feel" you and tune into your humanness and you tune into theirs, you can be successful with that person. Even when you make a mistake and admit it, they're more forgiving than if you remain at a distance or try to deny your error. You can't be successful without people trusting you.

✦ THOUGHT TO THINK ON ✦

You catch more flies with honey than you do with vinegar.
                                        —American saying

Insights into the Right Treatment

1. Look for the humanness in people.
2. When you let people know you need them, usually they're more than happy to help you.
3. Treat others as you would like to be treated.

THE RIGHT CREATIVITY

There is a term in psychology known as "functional fixedness." Basically it means seeing an object as useful only for its common purpose. For example, one may see an apple as food and consider that as its only purpose. But think about all of the other uses of an apple: beauty products, holistic remedies, trees (shade, oxygen), Christmas wreaths—the list goes on. Imagine if, when the apple fell and hit Sir Isaac Newton on the head, he merely picked it up, dusted it off, and ate it? If he saw the apple only as food, he would have never discovered gravity.

Creativity is one of the most significant talents of an entrepreneur. Where would I be if I had been functionally fixed on radio advertising? Suppose that when I called the advertising director at the radio station, he told me the high cost of advertising and I thought of buying advertisements as the only way to market on radio? I would have thanked him for his time, hung up, and gone back to selling and hauling those Bibles door-to-door.

Many people have told me that they admire my success because I fought "the odds" and won. One of the many odds, I am told, was that I was "so young." However, I attribute my success to the fact that I *was* a child at the time, and I have retained some of that childlike manner because I see it as beneficial. Children do not see things as they are. They only see what they want and the outcomes of their actions.

When I was a little girl, there was a great snowstorm one night. The next morning, the neighborhood children flocked to the surrounding hills in Pittsburgh with their toboggans and wooden sleds. My parents barely had money for shoes, let alone luxury items like sleds. But that didn't stop my brothers and me from joining in on the fun of "sledding." We went to the supermarket and got large empty cardboard boxes and turned them into sleds. Our makeshift sleds worked just fine, and we had a ball. The point is, our goal was to get down the hills on something, and we did. After the sledding was over, I reminded my brothers that the other advantage that we had was that we didn't have to lug our sleds home and put them away; we had only to look for the nearest trash bin.

When you don't have money, you must be creative, whether it's coming up with a unique marketing approach or playing in the snow. In order to be creative, you must rekindle the child in you, relax, and do nothing. Yes, nothing. Relieving your mind of burdens will allow your creativity to flow.

Most of us have forgotten how to relax, are almost ashamed to do nothing, and rarely are caught playing. While writing this book, I would often stop and switch the computer to an ongoing game of solitaire. You can't imagine how many people would see me playing solitaire and inquire as to why I had nothing better to do. Both play and relaxation are a significant part of the creative cycle. Play is what relieves us of our burdens so that we can relax and be creative.

Thinking like a child is imperative to being creative, whether it's relaxing, playing, or getting something that you want. When children want something, it never crosses their minds that they can't have it. Bill Cosby has a comedy special in which he talks about his two-year-old child wanting a cookie. He goes into elaborate detail on how the child is told that she can't have a cookie. Subsequently, he places the cookie jar on a high shelf, far out of the toddler's reach. Lo and behold, Bill walks into the kitchen a little while later and discovers that the child has built a makeshift ladder out of chairs and boxes and has gained access to the cookie jar. The child found a way to get the cookie even though she was told she couldn't have one. When she looked up at the cookie jar, which was deliberately placed out of her reach, she didn't see impossibility. Instead, she looked around her at things on her level and saw opportunity.

Children dismiss what society says about the word *no*. They rarely say, "Okay," when told they can't have something; they ask, "Why not?" Remember my story about the Buster Brown shoes and being told I couldn't have them? I didn't walk away quietly. When my mother said no, I asked my father. When he said no, I found a way to get the shoes on my own, by making my own money.

✦ THOUGHT TO THINK ON ✦

Don't think! Thinking is the enemy of creativity.

—Ray Bradbury

Insights into Creativity

1. Creativity is essential to the entrepreneur.
2. Take time to relax and enjoy yourself. Only then will your creative juices start to flow.
3. Play. Playing relieves us of stress.

THE COMPETITION

There's an old saying from India that goes, "You never step in the same water twice." My guess is that it means that nothing remains the same, that nothing is stagnant. Each moment is different, each snowflake is different, and each person is different. There is a lot of talk about watching the competition, checking them out to see what they're doing. Whatever the competition is doing, you can't duplicate it. If you both hired the same marketing firm and had the same public-relations consultant and that person gave both you and the competition the exact same recipe for success, most likely you would each proceed differently. Why? Because no two people or situations are the same.

If you focus your attention on the steps I've mentioned and remember to treat all of your clients and customers with care, you will have little or no time to concern yourself with the company down the street. I prefer, in most cases, to see other like businesses as my colleagues, not my competitors. Thinking in this way allows me to keep the doors of creativity open for my own business success. Work to develop unique ideas that will put your personal stamp on your business. When you do, you will build a name for your company that says, "My service or product is like no other."

✦ THOUGHT TO THINK ON ✦

The successful entrepreneur sells his goods on their merit—not by knocking his competitors.

Insights into the Competition

1. We are all different. You can't duplicate what the competition is doing.
2. Don't spend a lot of time worrying about the competition. Let your creativity lead you toward being unique. You will definitely win the race if you are the only one in it.

IF YOU NEED IT, ASK FOR IT

It's important to be able to ask for what you want and need. Only when you articulate your needs and wants can you receive the necessary assistance. The benefit from asking for what you want is that you will get it. By now you are saying, "Hey, just a minute. I've asked plenty of people for help, support, or information, and they are either evasive or refuse to be helpful." Well, guess what? I know those people exist because I have met them, too. Encountering them can make us shy away from asking for anything. We then agonize over our concerns or ideas because we don't want to appear foolish or less than perfect in other people's eyes. But I also know that there are people who *want* to help and *do*. If they don't beat a path to our door, we should make it our business to seek them out.

Shortly after starting the travel agency, I searched every place I could think of for books and information that would help me build my business. I kept hitting dead ends. Then I remembered hearing about a couple who were interested in starting a travel company. I managed to get the phone number of the couple and called them, thinking I might be able to get some help.

I called, and the wife answered. I told her my name and that I had several successful bus tours under my belt and wanted to know if there was any advice that she could offer that would help me. The woman, in an unfriendly manner, told me that she was familiar with my tours and that she had no intention of helping me, since that might jeopardize her and her husband's business. She promptly suggested that I not bother her again and hung up the phone.

For a couple of weeks after the incident I was hesitant to call anyone I didn't know. Then it finally dawned on me that anyone who could help me with the business would have to be someone I didn't know. After all, no one I knew even had a business.

Of all of the independently owned travel companies in the country at that time, the Henderson Travel Agency in Atlanta, Georgia, was probably the most famous. I had read about the company in travel trade magazines, *Ebony* magazine, and even our own local newspaper. After convincing myself that there had to be someone who would take a different attitude than the first woman, I took a leap of faith and called Freddie Henderson, owner of the travel company. And I'm glad I did. Mrs. Henderson took the time to explain the travel business to me, the best way to get repeat business, and how to go about advertising and selling tours to Africa and other overseas destinations. More importantly, she gave me a valuable piece of business advice. As we were about to hang up, I asked her if there was anything else that she thought I should be aware of. She responded, "Make sure that you make every person that you come into contact with feel important. If you do that, profit will take care of itself."

In reflection, I think the first woman wasn't certain how to run a successful business herself and therefore viewed me as a threat. Not surprisingly, her business never made it. Mrs. Henderson, on the other hand, was a secure businesswoman who had much to offer. That experience taught me to ask for what you want from people who can offer you information.

✦ THOUGHT TO THINK ON ✦

When you see a turtle sitting on a fence, keep in mind that he didn't get there by himself.

—Unknown

Insights into Asking for Help

1. Put your pride away. It can do more harm than good.
2. Before asking for help, try to know just *what* you need.
3. If you don't know what you need, participate in conversations with interesting people to spark ideas or help identify that which may not be apparent to you.
4. Follow the example of small children. They're *never* afraid to ask for anything!

BELIEVE IN YOURSELF

One of the most outstanding gifts you can give yourself is believing in yourself. It helps you gain and sustain strength to move mountains. When you believe in yourself, you will trust your instincts and feelings. Respect yourself by taking care of your body, mind, and emotions and live by a high set of standards and values. In fact, it is the ability to attain these qualities that allows us to recognize them in others. However, lack of love and approval, being compared to others, encountering people who put you down when you are already feeling bad, or thinking that you are not important or valuable can make believing in yourself and trusting your ideas and decisions a daunting task. There are times when the people who love us and want the best for us contribute to our lack of belief and trust in ourselves. An example can be seen in a conversation I had with a friend about his five-year-old son:

Henry's Story

From the time little Michael was born, his father, Henry, had visions of his son parading through life as a baseball star who would eventually find his way into the Hall of Fame. Michael, on the other hand, excelled in music. When Michael turned seven years old, Henry thought he would get things moving, and enrolled his son in the community's Little League baseball team.

Michael wasn't the least bit interested in his father's choice, and his poor game showed it. Frustrated, Henry told me the story and said, "The boy has not one ounce of trust or belief in himself. I don't know where he gets it from." Henry said that he had tried to get his son to follow the example of the other children who were better players. "Why can't you catch like little Leon," Henry would say to Michael. "If he can do it, so can you. After all, he's shorter than you and almost a whole year younger."

Little Michael spent most of his free time practicing pitching and catching with his father and still continued to fail miserably at baseball. In addition, he became irritable and difficult to handle at home. After the first semester in school, Michael's mother told me his teachers said he wasn't applying himself in school and was failing.

Henry was quite upset as he related this story. I know Henry loved his son and wanted the best for him. I didn't want to offend Henry or question his parenting, so I told him a parable that I heard once from Dr. Howard Thurman called "The Animal School."

The animals got together and decided to do something great to meet the problems of the new world. They organized a school. In this school they adopted an activity curriculum consisting of running, climbing, swimming, and flying. To make the school easy to run, all the animals had to take all the subjects. The duck was excellent in swimming, better, in fact, than his instructor, and made passing grades in flying, but he was very poor in running. Since he was slow in running, he had to stay after school and also drop swimming in order to practice running. This he did until his feet were badly worn, and he became only average, at best, in swimming. But average was acceptable in that school. So nobody worried about that except the duck. The rabbit started at the top of the class in running but had a nervous breakdown because of so much makeup work in swimming. The squirrel was excellent in climbing until he developed frustration in the flying class when his teacher made him start from the ground up instead of from the treetop down. He also developed charley horses from overexertion and got a C in climbing and a D in running. The eagle was a problem child and was disciplined severely in the climbing class, even though he beat all the others to the top of the tree by insisting on using his own way to get there. At the end of the year, an abnormal eel that could swim exceedingly well and also run, climb, and fly a little had the highest average and was valedictorian. The prairie dog stayed out of school in protest because the administration would not add digging and burrowing to the curriculum and later decided to join the groundhogs and gophers to start a successful private school.

Henry listened to my parable and said how cute the story was. A few months later, Henry invited me to Starbucks for coffee and a chat. He told me that he had thought often about the parable and had decided that little Michael should not be forced to do anything.

To believe and trust in yourself, you have to be allowed to do some of the things that feel right to you even when those choices made by you are not validated by others. When my business had grown too big for the house and had to be moved into a commercial space, I was excited. I wanted to shout to the world that after twelve years of having a business at home, it had finally reached a growth level that would allow for expansion.

I called one of my favorite aunts, who had just reached her seventieth birthday, to invite her to lunch to celebrate her birthday and share the great news with her. She listened intently as I told her about my plans to secure major corporate clients and grow to new heights. My aunt looked at me with tears in her eyes as she explained that she couldn't see how I would manage such a feat, since there were very few black Americans *working* in those companies and none doing business with them. Plus, she said, just the fact that I'm a woman is enough for big companies not to take me seriously. To prove her point, she asked me to name one minority of any kind doing business with a large corporation. I couldn't.

In an attempt to protect and defend my belief that I could secure these contracts, I told my aunt I didn't really know anyone who had a business that could offer supplies and services to the corporate world. We concluded our lunch with her reminding me that I should not invest money in moving into a commercial location. "Honey, it's one thing to sell trips and vacations to families and churches from your house; but the kind of exposure that you are talking about is risky."

I knew that my aunt was trying to protect me from what she called the perils of racism and sexism. I told her that I appreciated her advice and would keep my eyes open for the enemies she had spoken of, but I had to continue with my plans. I told her that if what she was saying was true, it was even more important for me to proceed, if only for the sake of my daughter and her future.

There are many pitfalls that we encounter that can make us question our beliefs and trust in ourselves. Filtering some of them out takes a conscious effort on our part. The method that I have used over the years is what I call self-talk. It's a simple exercise of programming or reprogramming the information that enters my mind. If someone says, "You'll never be able to make that work," I say to myself, Ha, you just wait and see how well it works. I told a friend of mine that one day I would be a guest on television's *Good Morning America* television news show. My friend responded by saying, "Do you know how many people there are in the world? You'll stand a better chance of being invited to the moon." I said to myself, Television shows survive by finding guests, and I'm as good a guest as the next person. *Good Morning America* called three years later and invited me to be a (you guessed it) guest.

When my aunt told me that major corporations would not give me a chance, I used self-talk to push pass her words. Before each business meeting that I had scheduled I would have a chat with myself about my incredible capabilities and skills. I would repeat to myself all the way to the meeting how happy the corporations would be to meet and work with my company. This system of self-talk worked a lot better for me than going into a company to get business with the history of racism on my mind; doing so would shatter my belief in myself and my abilities. Self-talk consists of the things that you play over in your mind to help you believe and trust in yourself. The next time you hear a negative thought or opinion that can put a damper on your self-confidence, try turning it around through self-talk and by reprogramming yourself.

I also keep in mind something my yoga teacher told me about how important each individual is to the world. He said, "If someone took a cup of water from the ocean, all the waters of the world would have to move over to fill the gap." Equate this statement to yourself and your life and it will be difficult to not have belief and trust in, and respect for, yourself.

Everything that you do in business is not going to be as successful as it can be if you don't have a grasp on the importance of good communication. And good communication should always start with a self-talk.

✦ THOUGHT TO THINK ON ✦

Believe in yourself and you will create a shield impervious to the negative forces surrounding you.

Insights into Believing in Yourself

1. To believe in yourself is to respect yourself.
2. Those who love you and want the best for you don't always *know* what is best for you.
3. Self-talk is a simple way to program or reprogram outside information to ensure that you stay on the road to success.

APPRECIATION: A SIMPLE THANK-YOU WILL DO

Sometimes a simple thank-you is all that is required to show appreciation to someone in exchange for a service rendered. While visiting a couple in St. Louis, the wife, Agnes, suggested that she and I explore the malls while our husbands played golf. When our tired feet drove us to take a lunch break, Agnes commented on how much fun it was having someone to go shopping with. She commented on what she called her "tolerance for salespeople."

"Doesn't it just burn you up? How many times have you gone into the store, spent your hard-earned money, and the salesclerk threw your things in a bag, never even bothered to make eye contact with you, and grumbled, 'Who's next?' What are they thinking?" I laughed and asked her, "When you approach the salesclerk, do you say hello to the clerk or thank you after the transaction is completed?" Her response to me was "But I'm the customer."

I certainly agree with Agnes that she *is* the customer, but what about the clerk? We have no idea what goes on in the lives of others or what kind of suffering they might be going through. Often an expression of appreciation as simple as a thank-you or an honest smile can be a turning point in another person's life. Remember, as an entrepreneur you are always marketing yourself. You may be the customer to this particular salesclerk today, but later on this salesclerk could be your customer. If that happens, what kind of person do you want your customer to know you as?

✦ THOUGHT TO THINK ON ✦

Kind words can be short and easy to speak, but their echoes are truly endless.

—Mother Teresa

Insights into a Simple Thank-You

1. A simple act of kindness goes a long way.
2. Remember that everyone is a potential customer. Treat them with respect.

ARE YOU LISTENING TO WHAT YOU HEAR?

"I know you believe you understand what you think I said, but I'm not sure you realize that what you heard is not what I meant." This statement is funny and can be misunderstood if we hear it without listening. All day long our ears automatically hear sounds around us. But how much of it do we really listen to?

Listening is an important part of the communication process, one that requires a lot of practice to perfect. Think of little children playing the game Telephone. That's the game in which children sit in a circle and the first child thinks up a sentence. Then he or she whispers the sentence to the next child, who whispers it to the next child, and so on. By the time the original sentence makes its way back to the first child, it sounds nothing like the original.

Why does the message become so distorted? It's not because the children couldn't hear one another. (Have you ever heard a five-year-old child whisper?) The sentence changes because the children are so intent on hearing the statement that they don't listen to it. They are so busy thinking about other things: how funny the game is, whether they will be able to understand the sentence, the other children watching them. There are so many distractions that the children aren't able to listen.

Adults behave similarly. Listening was not easy for me. Like the children in the Telephone game, a million thoughts would run rampant in my mind, which made listening to others difficult. Sometimes I thought that I knew what the other person was going to say, and so, to save time, I would interrupt them and finish their thought. This behavior drove my family and friends crazy. Or sometimes I stopped listening and interrupted because I thought that I knew what the speaker was going to say and was afraid to hear it. Whatever my reason, in time I learned that listening requires nothing more than just that. It requires no response, no argument, no interpretation, just listening.

When the true art of listening is used, we are able to hear what is being said and what is not being said. Listen all the way to the end, making no assumptions along the way. If you get caught up in thinking about how you want to respond or what you want to say, then listening becomes impossible. The mind cannot do two things at a time, so if you interrupt the listening process by thinking about what you want to say, then listening stops and thinking begins.

Become mindful of the two biggest listening obstacles: *interrupting* and *passive listening*. Next time you are in a conversation, test yourself. Are you listening to the other person, or are you merely hearing their voice and waiting for a break that will allow you to speak?

Other barriers to listening can be as simple as prejudices against the speaker: too old, too young, poorly dressed, not smart, too smart. The list of prejudices can be endless. Each of these barriers needs to be faced and dealt with in order to become a better listener (see chapter 2, "Overcoming Obstacles").

As an entrepreneur, you must become a good listener so that you can know the needs of your customers and not assume that you already know what they are. In addition, when you practice active listening, you gain trust from the people around you.

> ## ✦ THOUGHT TO THINK ON ✦
>
> *People hear noise; they listen to music.*

Insights into Listening

1. Next time you are involved in a conversation, notice if you are listening to the other person or just hearing them.
2. All it takes to be a good listener is to listen.
3. Listening barriers, such as prejudices against the speaker, can prohibit you from listening.
4. Entrepreneurs need to be good listeners to know what their customers' needs are.

BECOME A GOOD CONVERSATIONALIST

If you want to jump-start your creative energy and develop innovative ideas, then spend time chatting with interesting people. They are not hard to find. Before you go out searching for them, make certain that you are a good conversationalist. Start by asking people about themselves. One day I was taking a morning walk in the park and met Beverly, a woman who owned an auto-repair shop, had received a degree in theology, and studies Russian history and the language as a hobby and was eager to tell me all about herself. I invited her to lunch! During our lunch Beverly told me that she was a member of a local Russian-language club and invited me to a tea that they were having. Out of curiosity I went, and while I was meeting and mingling with her friends, the conversation turned to travel. By the end of the event several people expressed an interest in traveling to Russia. A few weeks after the tea, Beverly called me to make arrangements for sixteen club members to travel to Russia.

When an entrepreneur is a good conversationalist and can stimulate interesting people to talk about themselves, it leads to boundless ideas—and business, too. Most people have something different and interesting about themselves. We have to look for it. Let's see what Mary did:

Mary's Story

At nineteen years old, Mary Shelley wrote a literary classic. She got the idea one stormy night when she and her husband, poet Percy Bysshe Shelley, were hosting a party attended by several writers and a scientist. Mary engaged the scientist in a conversation about his field and asked several questions about human biology, which led to a discussion of the possibility of bringing the dead back to life. Their discussion continued over a period of time, and soon after, Mary wrote Frankenstein.

Where would the world be if Mary had been too self-absorbed and not curious about her guest? It's safe to say that the world would be without a great literary classic and Boris Karloff, the actor who portrayed Frankenstein in the movie, would've probably died an unknown truck driver from England.

Successful people know that they don't have all the answers, and they ask for help when it's needed. Sometimes we get information from people who have succeeded in areas that interest us. Sometimes we consult trade publications to learn who's doing things that will help us in our business. And sometimes listening to people who have led interesting lives can be just the thing we need. Don't be afraid to talk to them.

✦ THOUGHT TO THINK ON ✦

Good communication is as stimulating as black coffee, and just as hard to sleep after.

—Anne Morrow Lindbergh

Insights into Conversationalists

1. Spend time with interesting people to jump-start your creative energy and get new ideas.
2. The lives of interesting people can sometimes show us what we need.
3. Being a good conversationalist is a good way to develop customers and clients.

WRAP-UP

We intuitively know the effective way to communicate. However, sometimes it gets lost when we don't live and think deliberately. Create the kinds of habits that allow you to recognize the significance of moving into another person's space, of understanding who they are and where they are coming from. Whether we are looking for the right product or service, searching for our target market, or dealing with friends or family, we are dealing with humans, and we need to communicate on a human level.

On looking back at the process of communication, we see that the right product or service, the correct target market, sales, and distribution are just a part of making our business work. We saw that presenting ourselves and articulating our needs, self-talk, and language are important in our lives. We've read that making the other person feel special and connecting with them can help us reach our goals. Communication is tantamount to achieving success in business and private life. If we communicate well, we will market well.

REVIEW

Choose the right product.
Find the customer through the product.
Be open to change.
Identify the **right people** to buy your product.

Be sure that the people who help you get the **right treatment.**

Make the customer **feel** special.

Connect with people.

Ask for what you want.

Keep a list of **wise friends.**

Rekindle the **child** in you to develop creativity.

Be aware and alert to your surroundings.

Engage in positive **self-talk.**

Practice the art of **listening.**

Be a good conversationalist.

Chapter 4

BUILDING A DYNAMIC SUPPORT SYSTEM

◆

The Bible business was booming. However, I saw two problems: (1) not everybody needed or wanted one, particularly for $49.95, and (2) few people needed multiple copies. There was, in short, little chance for repeat business.

My next venture came just before my baby's first birthday and has continued until today—the travel business. I didn't know anything about this business, but I did know that social clubs made money by selling tickets on chartered buses headed for the local racetrack. I knew because I bought one of those tickets. After boarding the bus, I became intrigued with the idea of chartering. While sitting on the bus, I did a quick calculation in my head: There were forty people seated, each of whom had paid five dollars to take the bus trip, totaling two hundred dollars. The club's expense for the trip was the fifty-dollar fee for the bus. The club had netted $150 for one trip. I BOUGHT a five-dollar ticket on a Saturday. That following Monday morning, I chartered my first bus and started SELLING trips to the races. In two weeks I had filled two buses and had already begun to calculate how much more money I could make if I increased the number of sales.

To expand the business, I rounded up a few other young mothers who wanted to work and offered them part of the profit. I wrote a sales script, and we rehearsed it until we sounded professional. The success of the Bible business allowed me the opportunity to afford a spacious apartment where we set up shop and shared the cost of a baby-sitter, housekeeper, and cook. We began calling people listed in the white pages of the phone book from 9:00 A.M. to 7:00 P.M.

We not only filled numerous buses to the racetrack; we booked trips for destinations all over the country. "Never say we can't," I told the women. "Wherever the client wants to go, we'll find the right way to get them there." Finding the way took fast thinking, hard study, and every resource I could find. In expanding the business we learned how to negotiate with airlines and railroads for tickets and hotels and cruise ships for reservations. Before long, we were booking reservations for people to travel all over the world.

Up to this point in my business ventures I began to notice that I had my greatest successes when I enlisted the support of others, whether it was by bringing in people to help me work or by seeking information from someone with experience. I saw this as an important process that led to my success as an entrepreneur. Then I arrived at the fourth step—**BUILDING A DYNAMIC SUPPORT SYSTEM.**

BECOMING THE BEST LEADER

There's an important philosophy about leadership that says: The best leaders are those who surround themselves with good people.

Much has been written about Ronald Reagan and how he was out of the "loop" on some rather earthshaking affairs of state. In addition, he was known for his daily afternoon naps. Yet history will long recall Reagan as a highly capable and effective leader because he surrounded himself with capable people. He put together a team of advisers whom he trusted, and they in turn helped him succeed.

A strong support system is the key to success, whether in the White House or in your own business. You must develop a support system that will build a foundation for success. Doing so entails putting the right people in place and trusting your instincts.

Your business can collapse around you without the proper support system. However, entrepreneurs, thinking they can do everything themselves, often disregard this process. The first thing to recognize is that you can't. Whatever the nature of your business, you will need support. The order in which you establish your system is not as important as making sure that it's in place. As you and your business evolve, you will see that your support system will also evolve.

You wouldn't eat only one type of food; you need a variety to keep your system running smoothly. The same premise applies to a successful entrepreneur's support system. You need many different kinds of people, such as mentors, advocates, coaches, and nurturers to build an effective support system. Never rely on just one person; if they crumble, so will you.

✦ THOUGHT TO THINK ON ✦

Leadership: the art of getting someone else to do something you want done because he wants to do it.

—*Dwight D. Eisenhower*

Insights into Leadership

1. The best leaders surround themselves with good people.
2. Remember that you can't do everything yourself.
3. A one-person support system cannot satisfy all entrepreneurial needs.

THE MENTOR

A mentor is invaluable in the entrepreneur's world. This is the person who will guide you. One of the most critical jobs of the mentor is to critique your work. One of your responsibilities is to accept his or her analysis. Many people get defensive when their work is critiqued and see it as an attack. You must be able to handle the criticism because, when given constructively, it will foster growth. Keep in mind that I am talking about critiquing your work for your good, which is not to be confused with criticism that is judgmental. Review in chapter 1 the difference between facts and opinions and in chapter 2 how to deal with criticism if you still have difficulty with this issue.

Mentors are not hard to find. One of the greatest compliments that you can give a person is to ask them to be your mentor. In essence, you are telling such individuals that you feel that they are successful and you would like to reach their level of achievement and want their help to do so. Retired businesspeople make wonderful mentors and usually have time to help you. Look for people in your field that have built strong, successful businesses. Many organizations offer mentoring programs and the Small Business Administration has a program called SCORE (Service Corporation of Retired Executives). Thirty years ago I found a marketing and advertising executive through them who guided me for several years.

Your mentor can help you by showing you different ways to approach a situation. After all, they have probably been through it already, and they speak from experience. If you are a new and young entrepreneur, you may be too close to the dilemma and lose objectivity. Your mentor can remain objective and help you avoid trouble. It's important that you do not choose a mentor who will sugarcoat his or her analysis. When a mentor has to take time away from the objective at hand to placate you, it not only serves no purpose; it is a waste of time.

Carla's Story

Carla's graphics advertising business was doing well, which didn't surprise anyone who knew her: Carla had devoted all her energies to it since its inception. She oversaw every detail, from the designing to the bookkeeping at the end of the day. She also acted as the business's PR person and spent many hours attending various conferences and conventions.

Although business was good, Carla found herself feeling less energized and unable to concentrate 100 percent on her work. She was puzzled because this was her love, her passion—yet she was not able to focus.

An older colleague of Carla's asked her to lunch. Over the meal they discussed various aspects of business. Carla asked him about "burnout." Her friend was surprised, for he knew Carla's energy level. He was able to give her some good advice: "Carla, it's time for you to find some good people to surround yourself with and take some of the load off your shoulders. One person cannot possibly do it all, or they will go through exactly what you're going through."

"What do you mean? I've always wanted to know and be able to do all aspects of my business," Carla replied.

"Well, that's fine, but in the meantime, what's happening to the quality of your work? Learn the art of being able to delegate; find some good people and let them do what they're good at. With you training them, I have no doubt that they will certainly be able to do the job as well as you can. This would free you to do the work you want to do and to do it better."

Carla took this man's advice, and needless to say, she soon found her energy level increasing, which in turn improved the quality of her work. This man's invaluable advice served Carla well.

When I was about sixteen, I used to go to a local dance club with some friends of mine to hear a DJ named Bill Powell from WAMO, a local radio station. Even though I already had my travel company up and running, I was still a little apprehensive about pursuing it further. I became intrigued with the idea of becoming a radio announcer like Bill. In fact, about five or six of my friends wanted to become radio announcers, too. Because Bill took a liking to my friends and me, he wanted to help us and would frequently give us career advice.

Bill knew that I had my own business and inquired as to why I would think about changing careers to work for someone else. I told him that I wanted to make a lot of money and I wasn't sure that the travel business was the way. He asked if I was making enough to meet my needs. And I was, but not many of my wants. "Good," he said. "Then stay where you are and continue to develop the business, and slowly you will notice your wants becoming your needs. In this world you have to have 'staying power,' the ability to hold on to your vision when things seem to be moving slower than you would like them to." Bill went on to mentor me through several difficult phases of a new business and remained my mentor until his death seven years later. Because of Bill's lessons in perseverance at that time in my life, he was the perfect mentor for me.

My needs have evolved over the years. Today one of my mentors is Cecile Springer, a dynamic woman who's a retired foundation president and the president of her own consulting company. Her role in my support system is to critique my work and help me remain objective in my views. Her unique ability to analyze every aspect of a situation has helped me avoid pitfalls that I was so close to that I couldn't see. This kind of guidance plays an important role in any entrepreneur's life. Don't build your support system without one.

A mentor supplies different needs for different people. Before you can find the right mentor, you have to KNOW what you need. And in order to know what you need in a mentor, you have to know where you're going. You need mentors for their wisdom, skills, and abilities to help you get to where you're going. Be an information seeker and ask direct questions and expect explicit answers.

Mentors are those people who have the information that you're seeking as well as the know-how. Rarely talk with your mentors without a pen and pad to take notes. Think about where you're going as an entrepreneur and how you want to get there. Write it out on paper if need be. Once you are certain about your direction, you'll be surprised at the number of people who will cross your path, ready to function as your mentors. There is much truth in the saying "When the student is ready, the teacher will appear."

✦ THOUGHT TO THINK ON ✦

Your mentor helps you to soar while keeping both feet firmly planted on the ground.

Insights into the Mentor

1. Your mentor is a person who has already climbed the ladder that you are climbing.
2. Your mentor is a person whom you admire and respect.
3. Your mentor's job is to be straightforward and honest and point you in the right direction.
4. Your mentor can introduce you to the right people, enabling you to reach higher levels of success.

THE ADVOCATE

Another brick in your support system is the advocate, the person who "blows your horn." The best advertisement is word of mouth, and an advocate gets that going. An advocate is an individual who is familiar with your work and has the kind of influence that can send business your way.

The beauty of advocates is that they are a very efficient form of advertising: They bring you new business that doesn't cost a dime.

The best way to cultivate them is by providing them with the best service and treatment. I remember one of the first times an advocate profited my business. One day, a woman called to purchase three airline tickets. What was unusual about the call was that she was calling the agency from another city, six hundred miles away. She told me she had met Lucy Stewart, a client of mine for many years, at a party in another city. Lucy had told her all about how well our company had managed her account. The conversation encouraged the woman to want to do business with us. She ordered three first-class tickets around the world, including all hotel, car rental, and sightseeing arrangements. The transaction took a minimal amount of time and reaped a generous profit for the company. I could have advertised for years and would not have found that customer. Lucy served as a strong advocate for my company. With advocates, your business can make money while you're taking care of something else. Consider Adam and Bea's story:

Adam and Bea's Story

After his company downsized, Adam found it hard to reenter a workforce with others who were half his age and willing to work for half his salary. Adam's wife, Beatrice, had been a homemaker all of her life. If Adam thought the job market was tough for him, Bea felt it would be even tougher for her. But the phone was ringing with nagging and irate bill collectors, and Bea and Adam knew that they needed a plan—fast.

As a hobby, Adam and Bea made wooden lawn ornaments for their yard. During the holidays, they enjoyed setting up their elaborate hand-crafted decorations around the front of their house: reindeer, angels, Santas, and Christmas bears. Because of the numerous compliments they received every year, they decided to sell a few of them.

They put a sign up in their front yard advertising the decorations. Then they went to work meticulously crafting each ornament; Adam sawed and sanded and shaped each piece, and Bea painted, pasted, and put all the finishing touches on each item. For weeks they worked. Unfortunately, the economy was in a slump that year, so people weren't spending money on extras. Things really seemed hopeless, and they only sold one Christmas bear—to a woman passing through town on her way to a local hospital to visit a friend.

Adam and Bea had almost given up when the phone rang. It was a friend of the woman who had purchased the Christmas-bear ornament. She loved the bear and asked Bea if she would be able to create the bears in numerous sizes, to represent the six members of her family. Adam and Bea fulfilled the woman's request.

One week after the woman displayed her family of bears, a neighbor of the first woman called Adam and Bea; she asked if they could make her an "angel family." Soon after, another neighbor called to have a set of reindeer made for her family.

Long after Christmas, Bea and Adam were receiving calls from people who could be traced back to the original buyer. Needless to say, the woman who bought the first ornament became Bea and Adam's advocate. The other satisfied buyers also became advocates. Advocates breed more advocates. It's a cycle, and this is how businesses are born and also how they last. A good advocate plays an important role in any business. Once word gets out that you've got a good thing going, it won't be long before people are knocking at your door requesting your services.

✦ THOUGHT TO THINK ON ✦

Advocates are those who remember the good work that you've done. Nurture them.

Insights into the Importance of Advocates
1. Word-of-mouth advertising is what the advocate does, and it's the most efficient form of advertising.
2. Go out of your way for your customers and you will have all the advocates you need.
3. A good advocate has the power to help you expand business in ways you never dreamed possible.

THE NURTURER

When Bill Gates wanted to drop out of Harvard to start a computer-programming business with his friend Paul Allan, his parents encouraged him. Today Gates's company, Microsoft, is one of the largest and most profitable in the world. Even though most parents spout words like "unconditional love" and "infinite support" when talking about their children, few actually practice it. Who ever heard of parents encouraging their child to drop out of college, let alone Harvard? Gates's did, and look where he is today.

Not all of us were fortunate enough to have Gates's nurturing parents, but we can start right now, today, and get the nurturers that we need to persist in our endeavors. The role of the nurturer is to provide unconditional love and support to help promote and sustain our growth and development in our personal and business lives. In order to grow and develop, we need nurturing at every stage of our lives. Spending time and energy dwelling on the perils of a childhood gone wrong is not productive for either our businesses or our health. There are as many different ways to get nurturing, and the nurturing that we need at one stage in life becomes different at another. Two qualities of nurturers are available to us. One is the more permanent kind, the nurturer that occupies a permanent place in our lives. This is the nurturer who you feel is always with you, giving you the love and support that you need. Sometimes these nurturers are parents, best friends, spouses, or favorite relatives. At other times, our nurturers take on a more symbolic form, such as gods, goddesses, or an old picture of an ancestor that gives you the feeling that they have the qualities of a nurturer. The Bible, mythology, or literature can offer a source for a nurturer.

Although I was only four years old when my great-grandma Denny passed from this life, I still have a vivid memory of her singing and rocking me to sleep. I remember her tender smile and touch when I would crawl up on her bed near the end of her life. If I had gotten into something that another family member thought required punishment, I would run to Grandma Denny's bed. I knew that if I could make it up the steps and just get inside her room, I would be safe, for no one would dare raise a voice or spank me in her presence. That feeling of safety and love has remained with me, and I keep a picture of her in my favorite room to refuel my need for nurturing.

One day, I asked my sister Helen, who also owns her own business, to share with me how she received nurturing. She told me that one day while sorting through some old family photographs, she found a picture of a little girl that had a very sad look on her face. Helen said she looked at the picture and said, "You look like a little girl that could use a lot of nurturing love." So she put the picture in a beautiful frame, and every night, when she finishes her meditation, she visualizes the little girl in the picture being loved and embraced and nurtured by her. The little girl in the picture *is* my sister. The mother in her nurtures the child in her.

The other kind of nurturing comes more spontaneously, sometimes from people whom we don't know or know only casually. These spontaneous nurturers are not sought out by us but are those people who pass through our day-to-day lives and say or do something that gives us a feeling of being supported, loved, and useful. And when you encounter this kind of nurturer, you will know that their gift comes to you from their heart. All that is required of you is to be open to receive and accept nurturing when it comes your way. Sometimes when we are not feeling good about ourselves, we close ourselves off from the good that surrounds us. You know what I mean; you're having a bad day, someone comes along and says what a great benefit your business has been to the community, and you respond by saying, "Oh, it's nothing." Even on the worst of days don't shrug off support; accept the fact that someone cares about you and your work with grace and thanks. This spontaneous nurturer provides temporary encouragement and acknowledges your competence and ability. Witness Paula:

Paula's Story

Paula, a good buddy of mine, holds a very powerful position as the executive director of an arts organization. Early in her career, several people told her that she wasn't "thick-skinned" enough to hold a leadership position. Such talk made Paula too sensitive once she assumed the position. She often found people taking advantage of her sensitivity by either "talking down" to her or offering negative opinions. Paula began to doubt her ability to handle the job. What she needed was a nurturer.

In the midst of preparing for a holiday arts festival, Paula received a call from an institution that she was counting on to fund her holiday exhibit informing her that they were with-

drawing their support because they questioned her leadership abilities. Paula was distraught and called me to tell me all her woes. Nothing that I could say helped. While we were talking, she put me on hold to grab an incoming call. After several minutes Paula returned to the phone with a complete change of attitude. The person on the other line was from the City Parks Department calling to tell her that his organization was told that she was doing an outstanding job and to keep up the good work. To show his appreciation, the city purchased one hundred tickets for the holiday arts festival. After that call, Paula became more receptive to praise and compliments from others on a regular basis. Even though the comments were brief and from strangers, they helped motivate her.

This type of "passing nurturer" may come in the form of a person saying, "Good work," "Thank you so much, we couldn't have done it without you," or "You're providing a wonderful service." Everybody needs positive feedback, and when you get it, it makes you feel more secure. The positive reinforcement gave Paula the confidence boost that she needed to ignore the negative comments directed at her and to realize the fine job that she was doing.

When we do a good job, the people around us will usually tell us so. However, we frequently only hear the negative. This can happen for a couple of reasons: Entrepreneurs tend to be hard on themselves and often aim for perfection. Passing nurturers are there to let us know the good that we are doing. However, you won't be able to receive their positive message if you are unreceptive because of a few naysayers. Remember, in order to receive, you have to be receptive; and receiving is as important as giving. When we shut down or close ourselves off, we miss many opportunities. A good place to start the practice of being open is to accept the positive when it comes your way. I remember a story that I heard once about an old man who had shut everything out of his life except the Lord. One day a great rainstorm hit his little village, the water was surrounding his knees, and another villager came by with a rowboat and yelled, "Get in. I'll save you." The old man replied, "You save yourself; my Lord will save me." The water continued to rise and reached the man's waist. Another rowboat came by and begged the old man to get in before he drowned. The old man insisted, "You worry about yourself. My Lord will save me." Finally, the water reached the old man's neck, and he looked up and saw a helicopter and heard the man when he dropped a rope from the helicopter yell out, "This is your last chance, grab on to the rope. I will save you." And the old man insisted: "I will not die. My Lord will come to save me." Well, the old man drowned, and when he arrived in heaven, he went directly to speak to the Lord. As the old man approached, the Lord looked surprised and said, "What are you doing here?" The old man replied, "That's exactly what I would like to know, my Lord. I've spent my life praying to you. I thought you would have saved me from drowning. What happened?" The Lord scratched his head and said, "I can't imagine what happened either, especially since I sent you two rowboats and a helicopter."

Be open and receptive to life; you don't know what kind of care and nurturing may come your way.

✦ THOUGHT TO THINK ON ✦

Ralph Waldo Emerson wrote, "A friend may well be reckoned the masterpiece of nature." I believe the same can be said for your nurturer.

Insights into the Nurturer

1. The nurturer gives you the strength to excel in your business.
2. The nurturer reminds you to feel good about yourself and the work you're doing.
3. Remember your need for a nurturer and become one yourself.

THE COACH

While nurturers may not know they are providing support and encouragement, a coach, on the other hand, actively works to cheer
you on and motivate you. The coach is upbeat and provides you with
the necessary feedback that you need to hear regularly. He or she
continuously reminds you of your past successes and cheers you
onto future ones. When you are down and can't seem to recall your
purpose or focus, your coach is right there to pick you up and remind
you of what's important and how the game is played.

In his book *Winning Every Day: The Game Plan for Success*, Lou
Holtz wrote, "Your motivation determines how much you are willing
to do. Your attitude determines how well you did it." Holtz, a CBS
sports analyst and former football coach, is a man who practices
what he preaches.

After eight months coaching the New York Jets, Holtz quit his job.
According to an article that appeared in *Investor's Business Daily*,
Holtz thought that he was going to fail as the coach of the Jets, and
he did. His fear of failure caused him to fail. He was unable to motivate the Jets and therefore did not bring out the best in his players.
However, soon after he left the Jets, he was asked to be the coach of
the University of Minnesota's football team. Initially, he turned down
the job, but then he changed his mind and decided to approach it
with a new, positive outlook and an upbeat approach.

After only a year, game attendance grew, and the team went to the
Independence Bowl. Holtz found that all the top players on the team
had conflicting opinions of themselves: "They all wanted to compete
with the best, but they all questioned their ability to play on that
level." Holtz's advice to his players was to not compare themselves to
others. With his positive attitude and motivational skills, Holtz was
able to overcome his team's doubts and encourage them to play up to
their potential.

Holtz is a true "coach." He is dynamic and knows how to help others remain focused on the goal at hand. Whether he was coaching at
the University of Minnesota or Notre Dame, he motivated and

cheered his team on. As a result, he will go down in history as one of the most successful coaches in college football history. Lou Holtz is an example of a coach who brought his motivational skills to play not only in ensuring that his team played its best but in approaching his job as coach with the positive attitude necessary for success. Holtz's story serves as a reminder that we can look to others for motivation and within ourselves for the acknowledgment of our winning qualities.

Having a coach isn't always easy. The hardest aspect of your relationship with your coach will be believing him during the "dark times," when he tells you to "hang in there" or that "everything's going to be okay." Try to keep an open mind. Remember that your coach is on the sidelines of your business, which can be extremely valuable, since he can provide a perspective that you can't. He can see when you are being manipulated or led down the wrong path by others.

He can spot your obstacles and hurdles and help you get past them. The coach takes us from becoming to being.

We all can use a coach in our lives. If you can't find a living, breathing one, try audiotapes and compact discs for motivation and inspiration. This form of coaching is a mainstay in my life. It is always there when I need it. I listen to at least one motivational and inspirational tape daily. And it's easy to enjoy a tape with your morning cup of tea or coffee, during your commute to work, or during your morning or afternoon walk. If you don't like tapes, many companies now offer coaching for entrepreneurs. Check with the business branch of your local library or the local chapter of the Small Business Administration.

✦ THOUGHT TO THINK ON ✦

Just as we seek mentors, advocates, and coaches, we should also try to give of ourselves and support those around us who are also trying to find or continue on the path of success.

Insights into the Value of a Good Coach

1. A good coach cheers you on and turns you around. Even when you're tired of the chant, your coach keeps on until you believe again!
2. A good coach spots the adversaries coming, sometimes before you do, and gets you ready for them.
3. Your coach helps you identify your obstacles.

PAID SUPPORT (PERSONNEL)

Paid support is another type of assistance that you need to make your life and your business run smoothly. Sometimes your paid support consists of people who work in your company: technicians, sales staff, clerical helpers. Sometimes it's the people who work in your home: the housekeeper, the gardener, the baby-sitter. Sometimes it's outside professionals, such as accountants, lawyers, subcontractors, repair people, or public-relations professionals.

One of an entrepreneur's biggest challenges is making the right hiring decisions. Almost everyone has made a bad one, even those who don't own their own businesses. Have you ever had a really bad haircut? Most of us can think of at least one; a bad haircut is usually the result of choosing the wrong person to cut your hair. Perhaps you put your trust in someone new, or you unwisely returned to someone with whom you weren't completely happy the last time. In return for your mistake, you're out forty dollars and left looking foolish until your hair grows back. As an entrepreneur, you're going to have some bad haircuts; it is to be expected. Realize that you're going to make some mistakes hiring people. However, each wrong hire will draw you closer to the right one, because making a wrong hire gives you the chance to home in on those attributes you really want and need for the position.

There has to be some standard of measurement. You have to get a good haircut before you can recognize a bad one. You must have a yardstick to measure when you are getting the best. Experience is a good teacher, and as your business skills evolve, you will be better able to identify quality personnel as well as recognize those that simply do not possess the ability to succeed. If you find yourself repeating the same hiring mistakes, you will have to stand back and analyze why you are hiring the same kind of person and why they disappoint you.

Sometimes hiring the wrong person can be funny in retrospect, but it can also be costly and frustrating to a small business. I know from experience:

My Story

I once hired a messenger to deliver airline tickets. One morning, because of the heavy snow, instead of driving to make his deliveries, he took the bus. He left the office at about 9:00 A.M. with a stack of tickets. At 10:30 A.M., I received a phone call from a woman who had found a stack of envelopes in the snow, just a couple of blocks from our office, bearing our company's name and address. I picked up the tickets from her and delivered them to their destinations. Eight hours later, at about 4:30 P.M., the messenger, trembling uncontrollably from the cold, returned to the office. His teeth were chattering so hard I could barely understand a word of his story. He said that after he had stepped off the bus and it pulled away, he reached inside his coat pocket and discovered that the tickets were not there. The only thing that he could think of to do was stand on the corner, half-frozen, waiting for the same bus to come around again so that he could check around the seat for the lost tickets. Obviously, I should have hired someone with better problem-solving skills.

As a result, I gave the next person I hired a problem-solving quiz to assess his ability to think on the spot. If we have a problem and our employee only has one way to solve it, we need a new employee or we'll have more problems than solutions.

There's no way of knowing everything to ask a potential employee, just as there's no way that you can walk into a barbershop or hair salon and know by looking at the hairstylist whether they will give you a good haircut. In order to make the right decisions, you have to take a chance. Even after the most exhaustive check of credentials and references, you must still rely on your intuition. You say what you want or what you think you want, but you're really only taking a chance. If it works out, great. But if it doesn't, analyze it, and the next time, as you gain experience, you can make a better decision.

What I've been talking about is an old bit of wisdom: Learn from your mistakes. Some mistakes can be both time-consuming and costly; try to avoid them.

✦ THOUGHT TO THINK ON ✦

Paying somebody does not guarantee you quality. Look for the subtle signs of a good employee. If you happen to make a mistake, learn from it and move on.

Insights into Choosing Good Personnel

1. Take the time during the interviewing process to be analytical, but don't disregard your intuition. Combine both in your decision-making process.
2. Present situations. Listen to the feedback. You can tell a lot from a person when you present "what if" situations.
3. Pay attention to details: Were they punctual? Were they courteous? Did they have a true interest in the position? Do they seem dependable?
4. While experience is usually preferable, don't discredit lack of experience if the person seems willing and eager to learn. Sometimes, a person can have all the experi-

ence in the world but lack the enthusiasm or other qualities you're looking for.

HIRING SUBCONTRACTORS

Because of corporate downsizing, there are plenty of folks hanging out their shingles as professionals and subcontractors. When considering hiring these individuals, make certain that they have the skills and experience that you are looking for and not just the desire to land the job. This was the case with a colleague of mine named Kevin who had decided to produce a marketing video for his potential clients.

Kevin's Story

Kevin made a list of the subcontractors that he needed and proceeded to hire them. He was excited about his professional finds, especially the man who would act as the project manager. I asked Kevin if he had seen videos produced by the person heading his production team. He said, "The head of my production team has won many awards as a radio producer and has assured me that radio production and video production are similar." After many hours of filming the video, Kevin and his team finally arrived in the video-edit studio. Much to his disappointment, his award-winning radio man had never seen video-edit equipment, therefore causing extreme delays and an extra five thousand dollars in wasted expenses.

Kevin now knows that before hiring his next "award-winning" professional he should interview and screen them and by all means ask to see samples of their work. Furthermore, the samples should be something that is exactly like what Kevin wants and not something that is similar to what he wants.

> ### ✦ THOUGHT TO THINK ON ✦
>
> *If you are picking up signs or words that are leaving you feeling doubtful, heed those feelings and investigate them. You haven't lost anything at the outset, but you could certainly lose a lot later.*

Insights into Subcontractors

1. Pay careful attention to words such as *similar, almost, sort of,* and the old familiar *Well, it's not exactly what we talked about, but I'm sure you'll like it.* Ding, ding, ding!
2. Always ask for samples. Don't assume anything.
3. Check references; then ask questions of those references.

FINDING THE RIGHT PEOPLE

How do you find the right people for your team? Most likely you'll interview applicants. But there's a limit to what you can learn from a first impression. More than likely the person who's being interviewed will be wearing their "interview personality" for that day. Chances are they did a little research about your company and came in prepared to tell you exactly what you want to hear.

The best way to approach finding the right person is to have a strong sense of your needs. Don't interview anyone until you're certain of what those qualities are. Doing so makes it a little harder for the interviewee to impress you with nonessentials. One of the best ways to approach hiring people is to write your needs on paper and keep it in front of you as a reference when you are interviewing. Finding the right people is more about satisfying your own needs than it is filling a position. Paul serves as a good illustration:

Paul's Story

Paul remembers with horror that when he first started his accounting business, he did not have enough support people around him when he needed them.

"There I was with a client, discussing their financial matters, when the phone would ring or somebody would show up at my office, and I had to repeatedly interrupt my client's time. It was awful!

"I thought I'd be keeping costs down by not taking on any additional help, but it wasn't worth the aggravation experienced by me and my clients! I actually lost business, because some of my clients didn't come back."

This is a good example of the effects of insufficient help. You really can't do it all, even when you want to. Something is bound to break down somewhere, and you don't want that to be your business!

The flip side of this story is to provide yourself with the *maximum* amount of support people that you can, as Paul found out:

"I began to hire a few key people I needed around me. First, I found a wonderful woman to come in and take calls, do some light paperwork, things like that. She was instrumental in freeing up my time so that I could spend that time on my clients."

Business picked up and grew to such a point that Paul also needed to hire another CPA on a part-time basis. This took some of the load off his shoulders, which again enabled him to concentrate on the things he needed to get done. Plus, it gave him and his business a more polished and professional look.

You can never have enough good support personnel. The busier you become, the more you will need people to lighten the load. The key lies in finding the right people. Don't be reluctant to hire part-time help, or if, like Paul, you have a business that is seasonal, hire people during the busy season. I have often hired people that I only need for a short time from temporary-employment agencies. They have the ability to provide your company with the most qualified candidates by prescreening people; all you have to do is make the final selection. Good help is the lifeline of your business. The right hires can take your company to tremendous heights.

After you hire the right people, it is important to step back and let them do their job. Much of how you make your support system work depends on being aware of yourself. Sometimes you find yourself doing everything because you are a perfectionist. For example, my father used to mow the lawn every Saturday morning. And every Saturday morning I would ask him, "Why can't Bobby or Pete [my brothers] do this?" My father always had an excuse, but the truth was that he really believed that *nobody* could mow his lawn like he could. But sometimes you have to understand that you can't do everything. You have to learn to delegate. Realize that perhaps another individual isn't going to do a task exactly the way you want it done—each person has his or her own style—but it's still okay for them to do it. And remember, usually the more people do something, the better they get at it. Moreover, the more responsibility you give people, the more responsible they become because they feel valued.

My daughter, Sharon, begged me to wash dishes when she was five, so I let her. Did she do a great job? Of course she didn't. But she did the best job that a five-year-old could do. More importantly, I wanted her to have a sense of pride and ownership in the household. I wanted her to feel not like a guest in our home but like a partner in the whole operation. This is how I want the people working at my business to feel, like a part of the team. And sometimes that means that things don't get done exactly as I want them to, but in order to get everyone to take pride in the "operation," I sometimes have to put up with some shaky beginnings. Each day that Sharon washed dishes, she got a little bit better, and so will your staff. We have to learn to lighten up a little bit and say, "Okay this isn't perfect, but it's doable." Also, your way may not always be the best way; you can get new ideas from your employees' different style. We can learn a bit about lightening up from Sherry.

Sherry's Story

Sherry had an exclusive gift boutique that was doing quite well. She had an increasing number of clients, for her product line was unique, and she made her own personal deliveries if the client desired.

Well into her second year, Sherry was finding that she needed to hire some extra help. She loved the preparation and delivery aspect of her business because it afforded her the extra bonus of personal contact with her clients and meeting new people, who in turn might be interested in doing business with her. However, she was becoming increasingly busy with orders and finding there weren't enough hours in the day to fulfill her obligations.

The time problem did not seem to go away, even after Sherry took on two support people. These women were capable; they took care of everything in the office that needed to be taken care of; but somehow they weren't lightening her load. Sherry had to step back and take another look at the situation. She discovered that she herself might be the problem! While her support people were very efficient and extremely willing, Sherry had neglected to train them in all aspects of her business.

So the problem was with Sherry. Sherry discovered that although she had hired two support people, she *still* wasn't allowing them to take on real responsibility. What was the point in having extra employees and not allowing them to help? She decided to step back and let her helpers take a more active role in the business. Under Sherry's influence, they soon learned how to do the job that Sherry did with the same amount of expertise and personal flair. Sherry's business grew and prospered as a result of her decision.

To this day, Sherry is thankful she made the decision to step back and allow her support people to do just that: support her.

"I never realized how afraid I was to let go of the reins a little bit. Now I can't imagine what I'd do without my help!"

Learn the value of hiring good people when it's time for you to do so. Ultimately, it is added security for *you*. If you have a great support staff, you will be able to perform your duties much more efficiently and with a clear mind.

✦ THOUGHT TO THINK ON ✦

Behind every successful business is a staff of capable and dedicated people.

Insights into Personnel

1. Choose people for their various skills; support yourself with people who have different skills.
2. Make a list of your needs before interviewing.
3. Remember, the better you train your personnel, the better supported you will be.
4. Once you have the right support in place, get out of the way and let them do their job.

YOUR SIGNAL TO OTHERS

Believe it or not, you cause the effect. Your behavior has a lot to do with how people react to you. When my perfectionist father mowed his perfect lawn, my brothers would have never gone outside and said, "Hey, Dad, we'll do it," because they knew that my father wouldn't let them. My father's behavior sent a signal that said, "Nobody else can do this as well as I can. So I'll just do it myself."

One day my sister, who has her own corporate landscaping business, was rushing home after closing her shop to prepare a meal for her husband and son. My nephew is nineteen years old and my brother-in-law is forty-something. When I asked her why these adults couldn't prepare their own meals, she responded, "Because they can't do it like I can do it."

"That's probably true," I told her, "but you must give them the opportunity; they might surprise you and themselves also." That's how people grow and develop, both in the home and in business.

Go over your operation and reassess what signals you are sending. Do you make the people around you feel like a complete part of your operation? Or are you trying to do everything yourself and at the same time complaining that no one does anything but you? Have you caught yourself saying out loud, "If you want something done right, do it yourself," then getting upset when your comment proved right? Remember, whatever support system we have is a reflection of who we are and the messages we have sent. Sometimes it's difficult to step back and say, "They can do it," because most of us are ego-driven. We want to feel that we really are the best, whether it's mowing the lawn or cooking a meal or running a business. If you want your business to grow and make money for you, then lighten up and give your support system a chance to function. Trying to own everyone's responsibility is self-defeating for you and unfair to them. A sense of responsibility helps develop character in our children and can possibly avoid your having a nervous breakdown because of too much to do. We have to let our children and spouses have some responsibility of their own. The *American Heritage Dictionary* defines the word *help* as "to give assistance to, to contribute to, to ease, to give relief to." It defines *share* as "a part or portion belonging to; an equitable portion."

Over the years, family members may have "helped" around the house; now we need them to share in more of the responsibilities. The key word for home support is "share." And that requires stepping back and allowing the people in your home to do so. I don't go home and assume that I'm the best bed- or bread-maker in the world, because I'm not.

When my daughter was eighteen, I got married. Art is a wonderful man who at that time couldn't cook. I had spent a number of years taking gourmet cooking classes and enjoyed it tremendously; so for our first wedding anniversary, as a gift to him, I bought him an eight-week Chinese cooking class. He loved it. The experience opened new channels for him. His new attitude about food preparation led him to explore not the drudgery but the art of cooking. He completed the eight-week course and then reenrolled with two of his friends for another eight weeks. With a sense of pride, he began to prepare meals at home. In the beginning, many of those meals were slightly suspect, but we ate them nonetheless. With each meal he made, he got better and better, and today he's a remarkable cook and makes most of our meals.

Still, there was a catch. Holiday cooking was always important to me. Like my dad and his grass cutting, I felt no one could prepare the meals as I could. By the time the middle of November rolled around, Art, who was deeply involved in cooking at this point, had laid out the entire menu for Thanksgiving dinner. I looked at the menu and I thought, Okay, no problem; if this is what you want, I can prepare it. Except he had already planned to do it himself. Even though I was a little hurt, I could not tell him that he could not cook the holiday dinner unless I was willing to forfeit his regular cooking. I had to step back and let him cook. It turns out that my family ate one of the finest Thanksgiving dinners ever. Forgoing cooking the holiday meal was an adjustment that I had to make. I had to accept the fact that somebody else in the house could prepare the Thanksgiving feast besides me. I had planted the seed in my husband that the concept of "sharing" is important and necessary because it creates a sense of pride and ownership in the family support structure and lifts some of the burden off one person. My husband never says, "I will help you with the cooking." He just does it.

In business, we have to realize that sometimes our personnel *will* be just as good at something as we are, and this can be a blow to our egos. Keep reminding yourself that others' talents and abilities are not a criticism of, or attack on, you but an asset that can lead to company success and growth. Although this may seem obvious, it's one of those situations that can fall into one of our "blind spots" when it is happening. When it does happen, you can pacify yourself by thinking, I may not be cooking the meal, but at long last I get to sit back and enjoy it.

The successful entrepreneur knows the importance of getting people to the point of sharing and not just helping. And sharing can be more important. Helping says, This is your chore. I'll help you with it today, but don't expect it all the time. Sharing allows people to *share* ownership. And ownership says, This is my portion, and I will become responsible for it.

Sharing found a place in my travel company fifteen years ago when our cruise sales were low. No matter how many meetings I held on the importance of increasing the number of cruise bookings, sales didn't grow. One day, during a staff meeting, I announced a profit-sharing program that would pay fifty dollars for each cabin sold, the money to be placed in an interest-bearing bank account and divided among the staff at the end of every year. The program involved everyone, from the cleaning person to the senior travel consultants. Everyone started selling cruises; even our messenger sang the praises of cruises everywhere he went. The cleaning man convinced his church to organize a group of people. The travel consultants became more interested in cruise bookings. In six months cruise sales rose by 75 percent, all because the staff had ownership in the process.

✦ THOUGHT TO THINK ON ✦

Sharing creates a bond that unites one person to another.

Insights into Sharing versus Helping

1. If you catch yourself saying, "Nobody else can do this as well as I," get prepared to do whatever it is for the rest of your life.
2. "Helping" is temporary. "Sharing" is more permanent and lays a foundation for pride and gives a sense of ownership.
3. Lighten your load by lightening up.
4. Sharing is reciprocal.

SUPPORT: THE PARTS MAKE UP THE WHOLE

When building your support system, keep in mind that all the various parts must provide you with what you need in order for your life to work holistically. Your support system is like the inside of a clock. If one part, no matter how small, is removed, the clock will not run. From finding the correct motivational source to coach you to hiring the right people, all the parts should be in place to support the whole. Your support system means having a group of people on your team who can help you develop your business and enjoy living.

When I think back to my own beginnings in business, I created a support structure without even realizing it. I found several young mothers in the area who wanted to make money but could not afford to take full-time jobs because of lack of available and affordable child care. And I needed people to help me make calls to sell travel packages. I found three women who wanted to work with me. I told them to bring their children with them to work. I hired a woman whose primary responsibility was to care for the children and prepare the meals for all of us. Each woman was asked to make a contribution of two dollars a day for the convenience. The young mothers no longer had to worry about the care of their children and were free to help me develop a business and make money for themselves. Here's another example of how one person supporting the other can lead to a successful venture.

The Country Band

In my travels, I ran across a country band that has quite a business going. Like most entrepreneurial ventures, the band had formed out of necessity. The guitarist, Lee, had graduated from the police academy and couldn't find a job; the singer, Nick, and bassist, Jake, were waiting tables until the construction business picked up again; and the drummer, Mac, was a computer major at a community college, struggling to get by.

While every member of the band possessed a separate musi-cal talent, each also had a promotional talent as well. Nick and Jake built incredible sets and props, which gave the band a professional look instead of a garage-band image. Lee not only composed the band's songs; he wrote advertisements and press releases that he sent to various newspapers and country-western radio stations. Mac set up a web site, printed business cards, and along with Lee produced a band newsletter to inform fans of upcoming shows. While each member of the band con-tributed his nonmusical talents, the other members were al-ways there to help and learn. For instance, Jake taught Mac how to set up and bolt the sets, and Mac instructed Jake in how to check and answer E-mail.

Of course, there are times when the guys in the band get into arguments with each other. However, they are smart enough to realize that decisions need to be based on the opinion of that band member who has the most experience on any given sub-ject. The band isn't successful due solely to their musical talents; there are several musicians who are extremely talented but never pack a house. The band is successful because they have built a good support system as a result of the parts which com-plement each other. Having started playing at weddings, special occasions, and local clubs, they have far surpassed their origi-nal goals. The band is now so popular that they are headlining in popular clubs and opening for national acts. Needless to say, they made music a full-time career instead of a part-time job.

You have to begin by thinking in terms of building a support system among those individuals who can help you make decisions. Choose people who have more knowledge and experience in areas where you are lacking. Find people whose strengths are your weaknesses. Filling in all of the little holes is what gives you the whole. Even if you decide to do absolutely none of what your support system tells you to do, at least you've heard another side and can make an edu-cated decision.

✦ THOUGHT TO THINK ON ✦

When spiderwebs unite, they can tie up a lion.

—Ethiopian proverb

Insights into Support

1. A support system will let you develop your business and enjoy life.
2. While developing your support system, look to see how you can be of support to someone else.
3. You and your support team will complement one another's intelligence and wisdom.

MAKING CONNECTIONS

Building a support system requires making connections. In order to build bridges and open doors for ourselves as well as others, we need to make connections.

Doctors who study a baby's development have found that even the very youngest infants must be talked to if their brains are to develop properly. Each of us is born with a certain number of "circuits." As adults, electric currents flow along these circuits and produce thoughts, action, and speech. However, when a baby is born, the circuits are not yet connected to each other. Scientists are finding out that in order for the circuits to grow toward each other to form a network that can support intelligent thought, they must be stimulated and encouraged to grow. Research shows that by talking to a baby, parents promote the growth of that network.

The circuits exist in isolation. The child can't develop successfully until those circuits connect. This same kind of connection is true for your business. You must be able to connect circuits to be successful. When you first start out, you may be cut off from the rest of the world, or at least it may appear that way. It is important that you reach out to develop your circuits so that you can build a connection of "bridges" and "doors" that open to other people, and other resources, for yourself and your associates.

So how do you get started connecting? Once again, start from where you are. Your starting point may be chairing the church bazaar, spearheading a political-action committee, or even passing out cards or posters before a political election.

Anytime we get an opportunity to connect with people, we are reaching one circuit toward another. Thus, anything you can do to connect is important to your success: Volunteering is important, the political process is important, just going out to a cocktail party is important. Always look to build upon those connections you make with people. Get to know the man or woman who runs the newsstand or the person from whom you buy your morning cup of coffee. Once you have a connection with someone, keep it alive by dropping a card to that person during the holidays or by making note of their birthday or anniversary. Sometimes saying something nice about the person's wife, husband, children, or parents is all that's necessary to stay connected. Let's take a look at Jackie and how she connected her circuits:

Jackie's Story

Jackie, owner of a successful computer training company, said that it all started for her at a backyard cookout. At the time, Jackie was new to the entrepreneurial world and had very little money to advertise, so she made it a habit to connect with as many people as she could in hopes of spreading the word about her company. At a Fourth of July cookout at the home of some friends, Jackie met Hank, a lawyer who was a political candidate running for a seat on the court of common pleas. Hank was in need of volunteers to help with his political race. Jackie had never been involved in politics but agreed that she would join his committee. Over the course of several weeks, *while working as a volunteer for Hank, Jackie met several people who became clients of her computer-program-training business. The big break came for Jackie when one of Hank's supporters held a fund-raiser for his campaign and Jackie went to help out. During a conversation between the host and one of the contacts that had become Jackie's client, the host asked to be introduced to Jackie. It turns out that the host of the party was a president of a large corporation and asked Jackie to come by his office to meet the woman in charge of their computer department, for they were in need of a trainer. The meeting resulted in Jackie's landing a $250,000 contract with the company. That contract opened the doors to several other sizable contracts. Two years later, Jackie was made an offer by a larger concern to buy her company. Jackie never told me exactly what she sold the company for, but she said that it was enough to give her a long break—during which she took a trip around the world—before starting her next business.*

Keep connecting your circuits and see how far you can go. Keeping in touch helps you stay connected. Sometimes just calling people and asking for their help can solidify relationships. People love to be asked for assistance. It makes them feel good about themselves when they are helping other people.

The successful entrepreneur remembers that connecting is never a one-way street. So when we are making connections, we are not just doing it for ourselves; we are connecting with each other. I've been able to tap into the resources and energy of other talented people. In turn, I've allowed them to tap into mine.

✦ THOUGHT TO THINK ON ✦

Making connections leads the way toward making progress.

Insights into Getting Connected

1. Get involved in community activities and charities.
2. Join a special-interest group, such as a church, a social club, or even an exercise class.
3. Invite to lunch an interesting person you've met casually.
4. Become active in a professional organization, such as the Rotary Club.
5. Keep your connections alive by sending notes, cards, and E-mail.

SELF-SUPPORT: INTUITION

We all need support from others, but we also have to be able to rely on ourselves and, most importantly, on our intuition. Intuition is a "gut instinct," or a sixth sense. Whatever we call it, it's that inner voice that we must trust to answer the questions that we ask of ourselves.

Policemen are notorious for relying on intuition. If a detective didn't have "hunches" about a case, he would have no avenues to pursue. He wouldn't be able to solve crimes (or any other problem, for that matter).

Ted Bundy was caught when he was pulled over for a speeding ticket. Just think how many more innocent women would have been murdered if the officer who stopped him had written Bundy a ticket and sent him on his way. Fortunately, the officer didn't do that. He checked the car because Bundy gave him a bad feeling. It was during the car search that the officer discovered the tools of torture from Bundy's murderous trade and he was arrested.

Intuitive skills are mandatory in the entrepreneurial world. Every day as an entrepreneur you find yourself making spot decisions and facing challenges. You often don't have time to call around and get advice from friends and colleagues. You must use your intuition to help guide you. There are also times when your intuition can lead you in the direction of becoming a successful entrepreneur, as you will see from the following story:

Dean's Story

At age forty-seven, a severe viral infection left Dean Rinella partially paralyzed. Due to his condition, he was no longer able to work. As part of his physical therapy, it was suggested that he spend time using his personal computer to help him regain use of his hands. In the past, Dean had enjoyed the challenge of using the computer and had worked hard to perfect his skills. He had especially enjoyed surfing the Internet.

Due to his disability, the Internet became even more important to him. It was now his only means of leaving his home, enabling him to artificially travel outside the boundaries imposed on him by his condition. Spending a great deal of time on the net led him to become interested in creating his own web page. Dean found that creating his web-site design was challenging to his technical skills, and he enjoyed the creativity involved in the design process. He intended the site as a means to make contact and exchange ideas with others who were in the same situation as he.

As he became more accomplished at web creation, he began looking at the other web sites that he visited with a more critical eye. There was one site that he visited often and especially enjoyed, but he began to notice that several of the site's links were no longer current and the page itself was not being updated as often as it once had been.

Acting on a hunch, Dean contacted the web master of the page, and while complimenting him on how much he enjoyed his site, he also mentioned the problems that he had recently noticed. After exchanging E-mails, the web master admitted that he no longer had the time to spend on maintaining the site as he would like to. It was finally agreed that Dean would redesign the site, fixing the outmoded links and updating the obsolete information. The web master was so impressed with the finished product that he recommended Dean to several of his friends.

Now Dean has a thriving business designing and updating web sites. Using his intuition and making the right contact at just the right time opened a door that otherwise might have stayed closed and turned limitations imposed by a physical challenge into an opportunity.

✦ THOUGHT TO THINK ON ✦

Intuition is a spiritual faculty and does not explain, but simply points the way.

—Florence Scovel Shinn

Insights into Intuition

1. Intuition comes from deep within, from your true self, and when it comes, you feel as if you have always known the perceptions it brings.
2. Intuition is that sudden flash of perception.
3. Listen to, trust, and follow your intuition.

WRAP-UP

Let's look at the lessons that we've learned about the importance of an entrepreneurial support system. We've learned that the best leaders surround themselves with good people. We've found that mentors are very important to our business and that no business should be without advocates. We've talked about the importance of the paid support staff and how to avoid some hiring pitfalls. We've discussed how the family fits into the grand scheme and that helping and sharing are two different things. When building your support system, be mindful of how you present yourself. The messages you put out there affect the behavior of the people around you. Sometimes you want people to help and not share. But in most cases that's not what you want. You want your family and your staff to feel a sense of ownership. When an individual doesn't have a sense of ownership, you need to look at the situation more closely. Examine what you're doing; pay attention to how you think, to your attitude and your mindset, as well as that of those who support you, and to how they are reacting to you. Ask yourself, What message am I really conveying? Is that really what I want to be saying? Is that message the most effective one for me and my business? We know that making connections is extremely important, that any support system is reciprocal, and that you, and you alone, set the tone and the attitude for the effectiveness of your team.

I do believe that an individual can survive alone. With the aid of computers we can do just about anything today. Computers, however, can't hype our business, produce motivational support, or provide conflicting views or criticisms that keep us from becoming too isolated. What I'm talking about is making connections so that it's always a win-win situation. I'm talking about becoming more successful, and not by driving ourselves crazy or selling our souls. So I am not saying that in order to be successful you *must* play the connection game, but you're just making it harder on yourself if you don't. To dismiss connecting means that you're going to do everything yourself. You're going to be an island. Maybe you can be, but it won't be easy. Finally, we've acknowledged the importance of using your intuition for guidance and business development.

Successful entrepreneurship calls for a certain measure of symbiosis. You will draw from the talents and experiences of others, and they from you. Never underestimate the power of a friend of a friend of a friend. And as you build your support team around you, follow your inner voice, know what your needs are, and allow the team to inform your choices. Your inner voice tells you what is right, and as you begin to rely on your intuition, you will find that it doesn't fail you.

REVIEW

To be the best leader, **surround** yourself with the best people.

Your mentor will **guide** you; be willing to accept the guidance.

Your advocate **spreads the word** about how good you are and helps you remember your good deeds.

Your nurturer provides **unconditional** love and support.

Motivation and push come from your coach.

Remember to fit your family into your support system.

Your support staff is invaluable, so **choose well.** Learn from them.

Keep the connections **flowing;** they are priceless.

FOLLOW YOUR INSTINCTS. YOUR INTUITION IS YOUR "VOICE." LISTEN AND ADHERE!

Chapter 5

ACHIEVING BALANCE

✦

My journey from that first sale of a fire extinguisher to opening a travel agency and learning to trust my instincts has not been easy, but it has been quite an adventure. I had stomach ulcers, gained a little more weight than my small frame could effectively handle, and had periodic bouts with migraine headaches. Eleanor, a client who frequented the travel agency regularly and suffered some of the same ills that I had plus a few that I had never heard of, suddenly disappeared. Eighteen months later, she walked back into my office looking fabulous and feeling the same way. I barely recognized her. When I asked her for the secret, she told me she had taken up yoga and meditation. I found her answer strange and funny at the same time. Imagine Eleanor, a woman in her late sixties, doing a headstand. She told me that my ulcers, migraine headaches, and extra weight were purely stress-related and that I should go with her to the yoga center and meet Narendra, her teacher. I was skeptical; I didn't feel like adding a new chore to my hectic life. Over the next few weeks, Eleanor called or stopped by the office urging me to try her yoga class at least once. "Go one time," she said, "and see." Finally, to get Eleanor off of my back, I agreed to go.

The first thing I noticed when I entered the yoga studio was that everyone appeared to be much older than I. While waiting for the class to begin, people did different stretches, and it was interesting to see so many of these people contorting their bodies into all kinds of strange shapes, not to mention a few people in the corner practicing strange and unusual breathing exercises. At the time, I was in my early twenties, and though I had some health concerns, I felt my youth was an advantage and that I would have no problem doing what I saw others sitting on the floor doing. After a few minutes, everybody lay down on the floor and closed their eyes. The yoga teacher quietly emerged from a back room. In a very heavy Hindi accent, he guided us through ninety minutes of postures, very few of which I could do, to my amazement. I concluded that yoga wasn't for me. I thanked the teacher for an interesting class and told him that I would not be returning, explaining to him that I didn't see how yoga could be beneficial to my health. He was very kind and asked me some questions about what I did with my life.

I told him I had an eight-year-old daughter whom I was raising by myself, I owned a business in an upscale urban neighborhood, and I frequently volunteered my services to various community agencies. Fearing that he might try to change my mind, I quickly added that I was doing quite well with all of it and had no time for yoga. Narendra then asked me to assume the "tree posture" with my one foot placed on the inside of my other thigh and my hands raised above my head so that I would be balanced on one foot. I made several unsuccessful attempts, which made me even more frustrated and eager to leave. With a very soft and compassionate voice, Narendra asked me how I managed to keep control and balanced with so many external interests—my business, my daughter, my community involvement and social life—when I was unable to balance my own body in a simple posture. He said, "If no balance inside, outside balance impossible. If you don't like yoga and meditation, that's okay, you may leave, but should you decide that you are ready to live a truly balanced life inside and outside, I will be here, waiting and willing to guide you."

I left the center irritated because my ego had been hurt. Who was this man to tell me I had no control over, or balance in, my life? However, his words stuck with me all that evening and into the next day. I believed that I had a balanced life, but I couldn't shake his demonstration of how out of balance my life was. I went back to Narendra the next day, and he has been a vital part of my life ever since.

This gracious spiritual master taught me the fifth step of entrepreneurial success—**ACHIEVING BALANCE.**

HOLISTIC LIVING

Living a holistic life is to live a life of balance. The best way to recognize that you are living in balance is if you have a zest for living and get joy and happiness from life. Balance in and of itself will bring about a unity of mind, body, and emotions and the ability to integrate all of those hats that we wear and roles that we play to get joy out of life.

Take a moment and think about yesterday and what you did during the day and night. You will probably break down the day into components: showering, eating, driving, meetings, writing, exercising, cooking, shopping, working, playing, talking, paying bills, watching television, and sleeping. We tend to see our lives as a series of activities—those we *want* to do and those we *have* to do. And chances are we categorize these activities into two larger groups: work life and home life.

I'm going to suggest a different way of looking at your life—holistically. I want you to see your life as a single interconnected event. It has been a holistic approach to business and life that has helped me achieve and maintain a level of balance and success in my life.

Holistic medicine is practiced by both Eastern and Western physicians. A holistic doctor differs from a standard physician. The latter treats ailments of the physical body, and a holistic doctor treats those of the mind, the spirit, and the body all at once. In other words, the physician treats the problem as opposed to looking at the whole picture. Medical science is beginning to understand and better respect the benefits of holistic medicine. Even the most traditional medical facilities and research hospitals are beginning to acknowledge the power of the mind and emotions over the physical body. Traditional medicine is just beginning to understand that people must be viewed not only as flesh-and-blood components of a machine but as whole beings whose minds, emotions, and bodies are intertwined and interdependent. Think of your life as a whole event. Even though you spend a good part of your day at work and a portion at home, the two are connected. When we divide our lives into separate parts there is the tendency to allow one part to absorb all of your energy, leaving low or no energy for the other parts. When the other parts have insufficient energy, they can't get the nourishment needed for growth. Therefore, to separate them from each other is to weaken each.

I spoke earlier about my motivation for starting my business and succeeding; my daughter was the North Star that guided me both at home and in my career. At first it was a rocky road of complete imbalance in my life. When the travel business was set up in my home, I tended to overwork. I would get up at five in the morning and work until bedtime (midnight if I was lucky); in between I would squeeze in other things or combine them: cooking and talking on the phone at the same time, eating while writing at my desk, playing with Sharon while thinking and planning in my mind the next big tour, and so on. Finally, after realizing that a migraine headache could put me out of commission for as much as a whole day, my common sense kicked in and told me that since I would have to spend so much of my life earning a living, it would be wise and logical to figure out some system that would bring balance into my life. With my daughter as my first priority, I decided that I should not let my business suck the lifeblood from my relationship with her.

I achieved this by looking at my business for what it really was— the part of my life that fulfilled my financial needs. It was not my *total life*. It was a part of the whole. Danger exists when we take our lives and break them down into little components and give more to one component than another. And in most cases it is work and career that demand the bulk of our energy. This is self-defeating. Business is a *part* of life. How big a part depends on you. Earning a living, providing for our families, making a contribution for a better planet, and taking care of our physical, emotional, and mental selves are all important. They make up the totality of our lives, and we have a responsibility to each one of them. The easiest way to respond to these responsibilities is to integrate them, that is, to give them equal importance.

It's easy to get caught up in your business and career and allow that part of your life to outweigh all others. All too often we deceive ourselves by measuring our self-worth by how we make our living. The social climate plays a major role in this deception. Think about some social event that you attended. The hostess proudly introduced you as Mr. or Ms. So-and-So, president and CEO of the ABC Corporation. The person you were meeting displayed admiration for you, and you felt proud. You leaned toward that side of your identity, forgetting that the primary reason for becoming the successful entrepreneur that you are was to provide for your family, contribute to society, and realize your potential.

Several years ago, the *New York Times* published a series of articles called "The Down-Sizing of America." Their purpose was to determine what effect corporate downsizing had on America. Their findings illustrate my point. Through interviewing many who had experienced downsizing, they found families that had been split apart, spouses who had filed for divorce, children who had turned against their parents because the household money had been cut short, and neighbors who shunned the downsized person because the latter's position, what had originally made a good impression, had been snatched away, leaving him or her with no identity.

How many times do we meet others who start the conversation by asking us what we do for a living? When we accept and believe that all we are is found in how we make our money, we make our business or profession loom too large in our lives. Today it is fashionable to say that you own your own business, but that was not always the case. When I started in business, people were not impressed. In fact, people would often imply or even state outright that if I was so smart and talented, then why wasn't I working for some big corporation. Many believed that to work for yourself meant that you didn't have what it took to work for someone else. Internalizing such negative opinions can upset the balance in our lives.

How you think about a situation determines how you will function within it. If you believe that your business is all-encompassing, then it will be. If you understand that you have family or other responsibilities beyond your entrepreneurial world, you will live your life accordingly. This is why it is important to know yourself and your primary purpose. Once you can answer that question, you'll be careful not to let one component of your life overshadow the others. Our primary purpose should periodically be reexamined to ensure that it is still fresh, still a vital part of our lives. This reexamination will prevent us from getting sidetracked. If, for instance, you started out with the primary purpose of raising your children and providing them with a good education, and you find that your children are grown, have graduated from school, and are now leading lives of their own, it is time to decide on another primary purpose for yourself. Using this approach will help to keep you in balance and to live life completely; you'll achieve perspective and become an integrated whole. You know that work and earning a living are parts of the whole; so are relaxation and play, raising children, being good parents, being supportive and responsive and loving to our significant other, loving ourselves, playing a role in making the planet a better place in which to live, and giving back to the community. They all become our responsibility, and when all are addressed, they make up the totality of our lives. To prevent one of them from overshadowing the others is to recognize their interrelationship. If your primary purpose is to create a good life for yourself and your family, realize that you will need good health, money, support from others, and clean air to breathe. All too often we don't want to look at life realistically. We prefer to see it through the preconceived notions of others, by identifying who we are by what we have. However, if we look at life holistically, we will realize how each activity contributes to the overall picture. For me entrepreneurship became the economic engine that drove the rest of the train; it wasn't the total train.

✦ THOUGHT TO THINK ON ✦

The part can never be more powerful than the whole.

Insights into Holistic Living

1. A feeling of happiness and a zest for living are clues that your life is whole.
2. To keep yourself in balance, reexamine your primary purpose from time to time. It will help you to stay on track.
3. Remember, if one aspect of our life is suffering, it affects all the other parts in a like manner.

FOR THE LOVE OF SELF

To love yourself means more than loving how you look in the new suit that you purchased the other day or the new haircut that everybody says looks great. It means to love from the very center of yourself, that part that represents your true self, that is integrated and makes you whole and complete, the deepest part of you, as opposed to the surface aspects of yourself. Before we can begin to balance and live harmoniously with the world, we must strike a balance within ourselves that will allow us to love ourselves completely— and it has to be cultivated. I have found that the best approach to achieving balance and harmony starts with creating a routine by which we can order our lives. I often hear complaints about how boring life can be if lived routinely, and in some respects I agree. But let's take a look at one of the natural, often unappreciated, phenomena of our environment.

Every morning, just over the horizon the sun slowly rises in the east, *always* in the east. It slowly makes it way toward the center of the sky, never giving us any sign of being bored with the routine, and from there it continues its journey slowly westward until it vanishes and gives way to night, only to start the process all over again at the next dawn. This is the routine of the sun, never changing course, never varying. Between the time that the sun rises and completes its journey a whole array of wonderful things happen as a result of that routine journey. Flowers grow, birds sing, and life thrives from the energy of the sun's rays. All of this, from a routine journey made each day by the sun. Even when the clouds are covering the sun you know it's there because its rays bring the daylight. Think in terms of all of the things that you can accomplish in the course of your day if you start it with a routine that will nourish and fuel your entire day.

I rise each morning with this in mind. In yoga there is a series of twelve postures called the sun salutation that combine breathing and stretching exercises. Each morning I perform three rounds of these exercises and recite a salutation-to-the-sun prayer, given to me by my teacher: **You who are the source of all power, whose rays illuminate the whole world, illuminate also my heart, so that it too can do your work.** This serves as my reminder of how important routine can be and how it first brings radiance to me and then allows me to contribute to the world. Starting my day with that routine nourishes my physical being through stretching exercises, my mental state through breathing exercises, and my spirit through the sun prayer. From there I move on to other exercises and meditations in preparation for the day.

Create a daily routine that puts you in touch with yourself. It will help you live a balanced life by integrating your mind, body, and spirit. Think in terms of the total integration of these three aspects of yourself and select that which fits comfortably into your life. You know that if you want the body to function, it needs proper exercise and nourishment. I prefer the deep breathing and movements of yoga. You may find you like tai chi, qigong, jogging, walking, running, swimming, or some other physical activity that renders your body and mind fit. To learn more about life-energy exercises that boost vitality, read *Tai Chi Made Easy* by Robert Parry or *The Way of Qigong* by Kenneth Cohen. Whatever you decide to do, DO IT.

There is plenty to be said about developing a meditation practice. If I have experienced success at all in my business and my life, I owe it to the gift of meditation. There are as many techniques for meditation as there are people on the earth. Find one that you feel comfortable with. If you haven't found one to suit you, try being still and allow your mind to move into silence. When thoughts come, just let them pass and remain still and silent. The mind is stretched in silence, and this allows room for creativity. Give yourself moments of complete silence.

A good routine employs a systemic approach, allowing for total integration of the mind, body, and spirit. There are many systems and routines that are available to us now that promote health and well-being, from Deepak Chopra's *Perfect Health* to Andrew Weil's *Eight Weeks to Optimum Health*. Find the program that is right for you.

Select a routine that you can do every day and make it a part of your life. When making changes in your life, even when they are for the better, move slowly. Making drastic changes fast won't work; in a short while you'll find yourself back to your old habits. Start out taking small steps that you can live with. Take at least fifteen minutes for yourself; as time goes on, add more time until you feel that your morning routine can carry you through the day. As an example, start out the morning with five minutes of stretching exercises to activate your body and then move on to five minutes of deep breathing to energize your mind and cells and then to five minutes of silence and stillness. Or perhaps you might want to devote the time to reflection. The mornings are also a great time to recite your affirmations or give thanks for experiencing the dawning of a new day. For example, recite: "I am calm, poised, and patient; I have peace of mind" or "I am charged with new life; I am filled with new energy." Try the systems in the books that I've mentioned or others. You may prefer to take bits and pieces from each to create your own routine. Bear in mind that starting with the loving care of yourself will help you maintain balance. Like the sun, your daily routine will have a shining and radiant effect on your business and the totality of your life.

✦ THOUGHT TO THINK ON ✦

When you love yourself first, then love has been given to all.

Insights into Love of Self

1. Bring balance and harmony into your life by starting each day with a routine that nourishes you and puts you in touch with yourself.
2. Love and honor yourself for who and what you *are*, not for what others want you to be.
3. Being an entrepreneur is just one part of your life, not your whole life.

THE SCALES OF BALANCE

To make certain that we stay in balance, we have to watch out for signs that the scale is tipping. To start to balance your life and have a zest for living, the first rule is to slow down! Pay attention to the indicators: lack of energy, irritability, jumpiness, lack of concentration, physical discomfort, over- or undereating, anger, to name a few. These are sure signs that you are out of balance and harmony.

I can think back over the years to times when I have felt overwhelmed by projects and lost sight of the wholeness of life. Anger and lack of energy are the first signs. Such times are unpleasant and are a signal to sit back and reflect upon what is going on. Why was I out of balance? We have all been out of balance at one time or another. If we ignore the emotional signs, then we leave ourselves open to a physical ailment, which is what ultimately tips the scale and forces us to recognize that we are under too much stress. We live in a society that says, "Take this pill for this stress headache; take these pills for ulcers." Pills treat the symptom but not the cause. You don't eliminate the problem until you understand its root.

Being at the helm of your business means exactly that: You are supposed to remain in control of where it is or is not going. And that is a big responsibility.

As entrepreneurs, we have to practically live and breathe "awareness"; we have to remain aware of almost every passing moment. When we fail to do so, we fall into what I call a "waking sleep"—

walking around but in a state of unawareness. I have had my share of such a state.

I remember a period when my business started growing faster than I had anticipated. We were top-heavy, with a large number of corporate travel accounts, which meant staying open later and coming in earlier. And I had developed a side to the company that handled special events. At that time we had three large weddings taking place in Europe that required large numbers of people to be transported from the States; my company was also arranging all the parties and receptions. We had a host of group vacations to plan. I was also volunteering on five different community fund-raisers and was cochairperson of the YWCA's annual luncheon. I was working mechanically, without complete awareness. I often couldn't remember what I had eaten for lunch, or even if I had eaten. My irritability and snappy behavior caused an employee to quit just when we needed her most. Feeling, finally, as if the roof were caving in, I had to sit down and ask myself some tough questions and examine my lifestyle. What do I want in life? What do I want from this business? Am I still in line with my purpose? Am I taking care of myself and how am I doing it? I had become so busy that I had lost sight of balance and harmony.

After reexamining my life and my lifestyle, I started to make necessary changes. Upon examination of the business, I concluded that it needed updated technology that would make working easier. I also needed a few more employees. And then I turned to myself to get my life back in balance and rekindle the zest for living through yoga, deep breathing, and meditation. I said earlier that to make a routine become permanent in your life, start off slowly. What I didn't say was that sometimes you can be so out of balance and trapped into disharmony that your body and mind won't allow you to spend more than a few minutes bringing them back into order. I was so completely out of balance, the moment I sat down on my meditation pillow, my body would intrude in every way imaginable, from needing to go to the bathroom to wanting to scratch my head or continuing to move from one position to another. I decided that the best way to resolve the problem was to set a timer for five minutes of complete solitude. I

can tell you that at first it was the longest five minutes of my life. Today I live an Ayurvedic lifestyle and appreciate it. My morning routine takes an hour and a half, and I enjoy every minute of it. But it
didn't happen overnight; it took time. If you want more information
on Ayurveda, Deepak Chopra's *Perfect Health* and Harish Johari's
Dhanwantari, a Complete Guide to the Ayurvedic Life are terrific
sources.

We receive our own set of signals when we lose our balance. It becomes incumbent upon us to recognize such signals. By doing so, we
can keep our life in check. Holistic living means paying attention to
all aspects of your life: the mind, the body, and the spirit. Too many
times we don't do what is right or best for us. And when we don't,
everything around us, including our businesses and our families, suf-
fers. My friend Joe is a good example. Although he really hates golf,
every weekend he drags his golf clubs out to the course—because
everybody else is doing it. And then there's a woman I know who
spends a great deal of time on the tennis court, not because it is her
favorite pastime but because most of her friends play. The object of
living a holistic life is identifying what you need for a healthy mind,
body, and spirit, not what that guy or gal down the street does and
not what they say you should do.

You must first get away from what others say. You can accomplish
this by knowing who you are and what you want out of life. Knowing
who you are requires slowing down and asking yourself some questions. Once you know who you are and what you want, you will find
joy in life and prosperity in your enterprise. What others do will not
matter.

✦ THOUGHT TO THINK ON ✦

For fast-acting relief, slow down.

—Lily Tomlin

Insights into Balance

1. Slow down from time to time to see if the signs of imbalance—lack of energy, irritability, nagging physical or emotional discomfort, etc.—are creeping up on you.
2. Awareness is the balm for balance. If you can't remember at the end of the day if you ate lunch, you're living in unawareness and heading for trouble.
3. Knowing who you are and where you're going will make loving yourself and staying in balance a breeze.

SIMPLIFY YOUR LIFE

You may think that being an entrepreneur and simplifying your life are contradictory activities, especially if you envision the entrepreneur as always having a busy schedule and a simple lifestyle as being laid-back and easy. The truth of the matter is that thousands of people are happy living simple lifestyles. Many of them are millionaires who (you guessed it) are first-generation entrepreneurs. In fact, ask Thomas Stanley and William Danko, authors of *The Millionaire Next Door.* In their book they state that most of these millionaires reached their financial status *because* of their simple lifestyles. According to the authors' research, *self-discipline* is the key word they consistently came across when studying how successful individuals, most of whom were entrepreneurs, attained their simple way of life.

Simplifying your life is not that difficult if you apply a little self-discipline. You don't have to give up your city home and rush off to the country and buy a farm. You can start right now and where you are. To live a simple lifestyle, you can trade the material trappings for more freedom and less stress, quality instead of quantity. First look at how you spend your money. Do you buy designer clothes and flashy cars, support your adult children, buy all the latest gadgets, have to attend *every* social event? If your money is fueling one or more of the above and you are happy, skip the rest of this section. Simple living is not for everyone.

To celebrate my thirty-ninth birthday, I decided that life should become simpler as I grew older. So I gave up carrying a purse. The decision wasn't difficult to make, since most of the time I could never find things in it when I wanted them. Just searching for my keys was a major event. The final straw came one morning when the trash had to be taken out. To save myself time and an extra trip back into the house, I grabbed my car keys out of my purse, my purse, my briefcase, and the trash. I dropped the trash off at the curb and took off in my car for the office. Once I got there (a forty-minute commute), I sat down at the desk and reached to put my keys in my purse and—no purse! I ran back to the garage to search through my car, thinking that perhaps I had left it on the seat. No purse. And then I thought that it could have slipped off my shoulder and fallen to the ground when I set the trash down. I had sudden visions of my purse being crushed in the garbage truck's compactor. I drove at breakneck speed, praying all the way back home that the trash men hadn't arrived. When I turned onto our street I breathed a sigh of relief. The trash was still there! I jumped out of the car and rushed over to it. No purse. Frustrated and quite upset, I entered the house. When I walked into the kitchen, there, lying on the counter, was the purse. That fiasco was more than enough for me. That day, instead of returning to the office, I stayed home, cleaned out my closet of all purses, and took them to Goodwill. The problems that my discarded purses caused me were just not worth it.

Cutting back on spending is another way to simplify your life. The next time you go shopping and see something that you think you want, ask yourself first, Do I have to maintain it, dust it, wash it, feed it, or store it? Clearing away the existing clutter is another way to simplify. For me, my purse was just the beginning. The house was next. Then the office.

A simplified lifestyle means more freedom, which means more time. More time for the things you want and need to do to become a successful business owner and balanced individual. Once I simplified my life, I spent less time cleaning, dusting, and looking for my keys. Now I have more time to enjoy life and help others achieve success.

How much of what you do is based on what you think others expect of you? Sometimes the message is so subliminal we are not aware of it. Become aware of these subtle messages.

I was having a conversation with Rocky, my son-in-law, one day about getting a new car that he really didn't need. But that's okay. We buy a lot things we don't necessarily need. What was interesting about the conversation was that he wanted a four-wheel drive. I started to question him as to why he needed a four-wheel drive. As I listened to him answer, I realized that the Madison Avenue message that everybody should have one had convinced him, and so he got one.

Recognize what you need based on knowing yourself and not what somebody else says you need or should have. You have to be the creator of your life. There will be times when you must stop and ask yourself, "Is this really what I want?" "Why am I on this golf course, knowing that I don't like golf?" "Why am I at the theater in London when I would prefer lying on a beach in the Bahamas?" Are you doing what you want to do? What, for you, is conducive to a holistic environment? Or are you being kept out of balance because you are so susceptible to someone else's opinions as to what you should be doing?

Certainly there are times when we compromise and sacrifice for those whom we love, but doing so all the time can do you in. For example, both Art, my husband, and I love the outdoors, but in very different ways. He loves golf and feels that eighteen holes is sufficient exercise for him. On the other hand, I like to walk and hike and can't imagine that rolling around in a golf cart would be interesting. So we make certain that when we vacation, both of our needs are met. I like small social gatherings, and Art likes big cocktail parties, so we compromise. I go along with him, and he in turn will attend the kinds of social gatherings that I enjoy.

✦ THOUGHT TO THINK ON ✦

Do less and enjoy it more.

Insights into Simplifying Your Life

1. A little self-discipline will go a long way in simplifying your life.
2. Clear the clutter; clean out the things at home and the office that you don't use.
3. Simplifying will put you in better control of your life.

PREMISE: ANOTHER ROAD TO BALANCE

In dramatic writing there is something called the premise, the main idea of the story. All the best novels, movies, and plays have clearly developed premises. For example, the premise of *Romeo and Juliet* is that love conquers all—even death. This notion guided William Shakespeare as his characters progressed from first love to family rejection, to misunderstanding, to ultimate tragedy. If you've ever seen a movie or a play and left feeling cheated because you felt the writer didn't clearly delineate the characters or plot, chances are the writer wrote the story without knowing his premise.

This same thing applies to our lives. Knowing your premise in life means that you know who you are, where you are going, and what your reason or purpose is. It becomes the incentive to live a balanced and holistic life. To live within the framework of your premise you need a healthy body, mind, and spirit so that you can effectively and efficiently use your talents, aptitudes, and abilities. Sometimes we can become so focused on what is wrong with life that we lose sight of what we are living for. Bear your premise in mind so that no single aspect of your life takes precedence. Seeing life in its entirety will produce balance and make you a complete person. Know your premise and it will guide your whole life. Look what it did for Lynn:

Lynn's Story

Lynn Carr, owner of the Twainland Cheesecake Company in Hannibal, Missouri, is truly a remarkable woman. At the age of twenty-nine, Lynn found herself and her four-year-old son homeless. To make matters worse, she was illiterate.

Lynn's situation was so grave that at one point she took her son to a minister's home and returned to the streets intending to commit suicide by overdosing on drugs. She believed that if her life ended, someone would adopt her son and give him a better life than she was capable of providing. Fortunately, her suicide attempt failed. She said that when she woke up in a fog at a local hospital, her first thought was that she had even failed in trying to take her own life. In the distance Lynn could hear the doctor talking to someone and saying that they weren't sure if they would be successful in keeping her alive. Upon hearing this, Lynn thought about her son and decided at that moment to start praying. If God would spare her life, she wouldn't stop until she had her life in order for the sake of her little boy.

Lynn found refuge in a homeless shelter after being released from the hospital. She took stock of her abilities and skills and found a job in a nursing home as a dishwasher earning $2.25 an hour. She worked hard and long and saved enough money to find a small apartment. It was there that she remembered learning from her aunt how to bake delicious cheesecakes. She began baking them in the evenings after her job at the nursing home and on weekends and selling them to neighbors and local stores and restaurants. The sale of the first cheesecake gave Lynn the needed confidence to continue. Soon she began to receive more and more orders, and before she knew it, baking cheesecakes had become a full-time job.

As her business grew, Lynn moved her business to a storefront and began hiring other homeless women to help her bake. As the women cracked eggs and blended cream cheese, Lynn played motivational and inspirational tapes. While the cheesecakes baked, Lynn taught herself to read, and her workers spent the time studying for their GEDs (at Lynn's request and expense).

To this day, Lynn still hires homeless women for her company in an attempt to help them build a life for themselves.

Fifteen years have gone by since Lynn was homeless, and many wonderful things have happened to her. She faxed me a surprise a few months ago. As a result of her courageousness in pulling her own life together and her selfless efforts to help others do the same, Quincy University awarded her an honorary doctorate degree and gave her son a full four-year scholarship.

Lynn's early life typified a person who was out of balance. She slowly took stock of herself and developed a strong and powerful premise. She learned to know herself and understand who she was, and directed her life accordingly. Not only was she able to provide for her son; she helped others find the road to success. Even though her future looked bleak at first, Lynn said that her faith and belief in a higher power saved her.

✦ THOUGHT TO THINK ON ✦

Invest in the human soul. Who knows, it might be a diamond in the rough.

—*Mary McLeod Bethune*

Insights into Premise

1. Don't cheat yourself. Develop a strong premise by knowing who you are, where you're going, and why.
2. It takes a balance of a healthy body, mind, and stable and sound emotions to make our businesses run well.

HAPPINESS

According to the authors of the Declaration of Independence, "life, liberty and the pursuit of happiness" are our rights. This seems to imply that life and liberty are our birthrights and happiness is something that we have the right to seek. But just *where* can we find this happiness, and *how* do we go about finding it? Many say, "When I get that big client, I'll be happy." "When the bank gives me that expansion loan, I'll be happy." "When I go on vacation, I'll find happiness." "When I win lotto, I'll finally be happy." All of which implies that happiness is the sum total of doing, having, and getting, and is determined by something external to ourselves.

My belief is that happiness comes from within. No matter what we experience externally, happiness cannot be guaranteed. There are many paths that can lead to it as long as we allow it to happen and learn to appreciate each moment of our lives. Happiness is always there, waiting, if we only know how to find it.

Happiness exists everywhere and is present at all times. We just have to get out of its way and let it happen. To better understand my point, let's look at what can cause unhappiness. For example, you want to see your business grow, and you decide that getting XYZ Corporation's business will fulfill your desire and make you happy. You bend over backward and try everything that you can to court the corporation. It sends signals that lead you to believe that you have the account in the bag. You are so certain that the account is yours that you start to make plans to purchase new office equipment with the extra money you'll be earning. And then, wham, out of nowhere, the XYZ Corporation decides to give their business to another company. Now you're feeling the pain of unhappiness because you believed that landing that particular account was the key to your happiness.

Let's look at the situation from another angle. You desire to increase business. This time, you don't wait until one particular company decides to fulfill your desire. Instead, keeping your goal in mind, you call on many companies and make contact with many people. You advertise, makes sales calls, and send letters and proposals. All the while, *know* that if you want more business badly enough you have the power within yourself to make it happen. Within a short time, you find that you have acquired the business of several mid-sized companies and that one company twice the size of the XYZ

Corporation has called you to handle their business. Ah, now you're happy.

It may seem that in both these examples landing the accounts is what made you happy. But in this second scenario you achieved your goal because you kept doing what you love—running your business as best as you can. Instead of trying to land XYZ Corporation, you got out of your own way, went about doing what you do best, and achieved success—and yes, happiness.

We usually become unhappy when we don't get what we want. As I stated earlier, happiness is always there; we have to get out of its way and allow it to happen by accepting that life and living hold unlimited potential. When you know, believe, and trust that there are no limitations placed on you, you will be able to relax and allow happiness to flow, knowing that if you believe in yourself and your abilities, you and your desire will connect. To determine your desire is one thing; to limit where it should come from and how it will come is another. Placing limits on yourself and your wishes almost ensures an unhappy ending. How many times have you set out with an idea of pursuing something and gotten caught up with and attached to where it can be found and what it should look like, only to be disappointed. Relax and know that Providence will provide what you desire if you keep yourself open to all ideas and solutions. I have frequently found this to be the case in both my business and my private life.

When I desired a committed relationship, I also decided what that special someone should look like, how he should behave, and where he should come from. You wouldn't believe some of my finds; each one was a disaster waiting to happen. After much frustration, I decided to relax, get out of the way of my happiness, and trust that the best relationship for me did exist somewhere on this planet and that the universe would make certain that our paths would cross. Less than one year later, I met and married my Mr. Right.

The road to happiness can also take the form of the unfolding of your self-image. My friend Asha and I once talked about a friend of ours who appeared to have everything in her favor—money, popularity, and an executive position. Yet she never appeared happy and finally ended her own life. Asha and I talked about how important happiness is to our lives. Since being happy makes you better at running your business and your life, we pondered the question How do we find happiness and make it last?

Buddhism teaches that human life is the most precious treasure and that within each one of us exists the potential for absolute happiness. Thus, happiness is not something that we pursue; it's more like a continuous unfolding that occurs from within. We project it to the world, which explains why people who are happy attract more happiness.

That unfolding starts with us and our image of ourselves. When our self-image is raised to the point where we like who and what we are, then we not only feel happiness but we express it in our daily lives. I once heard a man say that if you want to destroy a person, figure out a way to make him not like himself. When you are not your own best friend, self-destruction and unhappiness are guaranteed. Sometimes all it takes to build a likable self-image is to reflect on what makes you special. In fact, make a list of those things and read them regularly to boost your image of yourself. When you feel good about yourself, things look and feel different to you.

Happiness can be experienced by appreciating how things are and how many wonderful things you already have in your life—your family, your friends, and the value of doing service for others through your business. Let's take a look at how this works for Mattie:

Mattie's Story

Mattie grew up in a poor neighborhood. Life was always a struggle for her and her family. They had very little in the way of material possessions, but they had each other and were united in a strong bond of love. Mattie felt loved and wanted and grew into a secure and caring adult.

She had dreamed of obtaining an education, but her parents didn't have the money. Mattie knew that she would have to work to pay for her education while attending classes part-

time. That didn't bother her in the least. Finding steady work was more difficult than Mattie had imagined, but she pushed forward. If one option failed, she would go on to the next. After eleven years she finally received the education that meant so much to her.

Mattie opened a nonprofit shelter for battered women. She wishes to share some of the love and compassion that she had experienced growing up and has been with her throughout her life. Although she is neither rich nor famous, Mattie says she is happy with herself and her shelter. Her happiness comes from within and shines like a beacon to all those who come to her for help and comfort.

Contrast Mattie's story with that of John:

John always blamed others for his problems. He had inherited a successful family manufacturing business, but that wasn't enough for him. Thinking that a big windfall of money would bring him the happiness that he sought, he spent his life gambling away anything that he earned, trying to make that one big score that he felt he deserved.

His relationships, like everything else in his life, all ended in failure, and he became lonely and more bitter.

Finally, John made his big score. He purchased the winning ticket in the state lottery and won a substantial jackpot. It was what he had waited for all his life. Now life would be different.

Always reaching for what he might win tomorrow, he let his business deteriorate; having won the lottery, he spent less time focusing on his work.

John is again just scraping by, having lost his windfall to gambling in search of an even bigger sum of money; through neglect, he also lost his business. Again, he is blaming others for his misfortune and is, again, bitter and lonely.

John had sought his happiness externally, never realizing that first it must come from within. The money that he thought would change his life never did. He was unhappy with himself and therefore continued on a self-destructive path.

Happiness is a state of being, an attitude about life and how we perceive the things that take place. Achieving it involves finding ways to get control of our mental attitude. It is perfectly reasonable to seek success, but before we can be happy with what we find, we must be able to appreciate our lives as we are living them, not always looking ahead for that elusive something that seems to be always out of reach. We must love who we are and appreciate the wonders of simply living. In this way, we can open ourselves up to opportunities and be able to find the true path to happiness in both our life and our business.

Perhaps when Thomas Jefferson drafted the Declaration of Independence he knew that if we pursued happiness outside ourselves, our search would lead us back to ourselves and allow us to learn the true essence of life and living.

✦ THOUGHT TO THINK ON ✦

Happiness is the fragrance from the flower.

Insights into Happiness
1. Happiness exists everywhere and at all times.
2. To live happily, learn to enjoy that which you have.
3. The pursuit of happiness generally leads us back to ourselves.

BECOMING A WITNESS TO YOURSELF

One usually expects to read in a self-help book a section about the old adage Hard work equals success. There's nothing in this book about exertion or hard work. I hope I didn't disappoint you, but the truth is that hard work does not equal success. You don't have to work hard to succeed; you have to work smart. The key to working smart is achieving a healthy balance between business and personal matters.

Many presumably successful businesspeople I meet complain to me that their children are getting into trouble or that their marriage is falling apart because they are spending too much time at the office. Common sense should tell them that being away from home is a choice that *they* made. If marriage and children were the first priority, then business would assume its proper perspective.

One wonders, If these successful businesspeople were able to listen to themselves talk, would they be inclined to change their situation? If they could "witness" their behavior, perhaps it would help them realize that they need to change it. In fact, before any of us can make a change for the better and bring our lives into balance, we must first become aware of ourselves, be a witness to our own actions and behavior. Management, like charity, begins at home. Before we can successfully manage a business, we have to be able to manage ourselves. A profitable business and failed family is not only unbalanced; it is hypocritical.

So how do you change your programmed behavior? Think of yourself as Arnold Schwarzenegger's character in the movie *The Terminator*, about a robot programmed to destroy others. The irony occurs in the movie's sequel in which the Terminator is forced to destroy himself. The key to saving yourself from destruction is to realize when your programming has you headed in that direction.

There are steps that you can take to reprogram yourself and bring about balance in your life so that you can live holistically:

- ✦ Get your family and staff to "share" the load and take some of the pressure off you.
- ✦ Outsource work to subcontractors. Often you find yourself doing work that is better left to others, such as bookkeeping, accounting, web-site maintenance, and proposal and contract writing, to name a few. (See chapter 4 and the previous sections Hiring Subcontractors, Finding the Right People, and Your Signal to Others.)
- ✦ Set goals within your reach. We can throw our balance off

by struggling toward a goal that is unrealistic. Go back to chapter 1 and review Set Goals That You Can See.

✦ Simplify your life. Review, in this chapter, the section with this title. Read about my decision to give up carrying a purse. No, I am not suggesting that you discard your handbag, attaché case, wallet, or anything else that you feel a need for. Just think about the things that you hold on to out of sentiment or habit that you can better do without. If you want to remain true to yourself, make your own set of traditions, standards, or values that are designed for your growth and evolution.

✦ Be an interdependent entrepreneur. Are you staying close enough to people for warmth, support, protection, and comfort, yet far enough away to keep from being hurt? Review the section Interdependence in chapter 2.

✦ Develop a "teamwork" environment in your business to maximize employee input and output. Read more on this later in this chapter.

In addition, once you have taken the steps that I have described above to reprogram yourself, it is essential to set aside time each day to reflect on your life.

✦ THOUGHT TO THINK ON ✦

Self-preservation is the first law of nature.
                                            —*old American saying*

Insights into Witness of Self

1. Step back and witness yourself. Do you see a person working hard while other important parts of life go unattended? If so, start immediately to put the necessary changes in place to regain your balance.
2. Self-witnessing keeps the Terminator out of our lives.

THE ACT OF INNER STILLNESS

In order to examine where we have been, where we are, and where we are going, we need to retreat to a quiet place within ourselves. In order to arrive there, we must start by creating a quiet and sacred place that we can escape to. If you have not already created your private sanctuary, start now. Find a space, an actual physical one, in your environment that is strictly yours—not the children's or your spouse's or the cat's or the dog's but yours. Finding it can sometimes be difficult; it is not unusual to discover that you have no private space to call your own. Create one that is yours alone, even if there's just enough room for a seat. However, you must make sure you find a *space* that is yours, in a *place* that is yours, and select a *time of the day* that belongs only to you.

Next, set aside a few minutes each day to go to that private, quiet place. Bring fresh flowers, candles, incense, images of your favorite deities, or pictures of ancestors into your special place. Personalize it with anything that embodies love, quietness, and peace. Start by spending a few minutes each day there and work up to twenty-four minutes daily in your private sanctuary. Why not take twenty-four minutes out of twenty-four hours for yourself and for your personal development? It seems like a minor goal and investment, but for many it can be difficult. In a twenty-four-hour period, sometimes finding these few minutes is like searching for a needle in a haystack. But you need the needle to sew the pieces of your holistic self together—it's important to balance. If you make the time a priority, it will be.

Once you find a place where you want to be, a space within that place, and a time of day out of the twenty-four hours, you'll be ready. Go to your space every single day . . . and just sit there. Become accustomed to your space and the solitude that it brings. Use it to review and examine your life; after a period of time it will become natural to just sit there quietly and contemplate, watching your parade of thoughts as they pass by. Don't react. Just watch.

Our minds and bodies need to get accustomed to quiet times. We are so busy all the time that when we finally sit quietly, the mind will start with Did I turn off the oven? Did I lock the front door? What about that account that I encountered today that irritated me? Did I say the right things to the repair person who showed up late? Did I say the right thing to my child? And that's after the body couldn't get your attention with itching, twitching, and other useless movements and reminders that you should be busy doing something.

Such reactions are natural. Look at each of them and then discard them. As time goes by, an inner quietness will naturally occur. You won't have to work at it.

Through the process of contemplation, thinking intently will allow you to learn more about who you are. Contemplation also gives you time to think about some of the things that you've encountered and the opportunity to evaluate them and think about how you really would've liked to have dealt with them or how you should deal with problems the next time they arise. It will sharpen your intuition. Plus, you are giving yourself a daily holistic healing of the body, mind, and spirit.

Enter your quiet, sacred space daily with no expectations. Just be. As time goes on, you will be able to carry more and more peace from your sacred space into your daily activities. Once you begin to understand your inner world, then you will be well equipped to handle the external world.

✦ THOUGHT TO THINK ON ✦

Expect nothing and get everything.

Insights into Inner Stillness

1. Bring into your private place those objects that embody love and peace and will allow you to experience your inner self.

2. Select a time of day that is best for you. Remember, the early-morning hours are quiet and peaceful.

3. Completely relax your body.
4. Once the body is relaxed, bring your attention to your breathing.
5. Don't attempt to control the breath; just observe it.
6. The slower the breath, the quieter the mind.

TEAM PLAYERS AT WORK

The same methods that you apply to your life at home can be applied in the workplace and relieve a lot of pressure. If you foster a sense of belonging among your employees, you may then expect them to share in the responsibilities of the business. Just as you must not be the martyr at home, you must not be one at work, either. I have an open-office policy that allows my staff to feel comfortably that they are a part of the business. They are not just people who have been hired to perform a function, but people whose decisions and ideas and recommendations are considered very seriously.

For example, if an employee makes a recommendation that I may not agree with initially, we talk about it. Often that person can get me to see an aspect of the idea that might improve the business. Sometimes in my questioning and answering the employee can see that his idea may not be a good one for our business. But the key factor is, it's *our* business. I am always apprehensive about anyone I hire who says, "*You* have a problem here. What do you want me to do about this account?" When an employee makes a distinct separation between what is *their* problem versus what they identify as *my* problem, I know he or she isn't a team player.

Team players are crucial to keeping things in perspective and in balance. They equate their own success with that of the rest of the team. These are the kind of people we want to cultivate. To be successful, we need team players on the outside, on the inside, and at home. Teamwork is important because it gives everyone a sense of belonging. Let's examine the following story:

Ann Marie's Story

Ann Marie has a very successful nail salon. In fact, the business turned out to be far more lucrative than even she had thought possible.

Like myself, Ann Marie found herself a pregnant, unwed teenager. With work options severely limited for a sixteen-year-old, Ann Marie had no choice but to rely on the talents and skills she already had in order to support herself. There was no time to earn a degree or work her way up to manager of a local fast-food chain. She enjoyed doing her own nails and always received compliments on the designs that she painted on them. She decided she would offer her services to other women. Through word of mouth, she began traveling to people's homes to give manicures.

About five years later, she opened her own salon, which had a small playroom in the back for her son, Anthony. After kindergarten in the morning and a nap in the early afternoon, Anthony would spend the remaining three and a half hours of Ann Marie's workday in the salon talking to the clients, playing in the back room, or showing off to his mother's two employees.

With the clientele of the salon doubling, Ann Marie was ecstatic to find Val, an extremely talented woman who would take over many of the responsibilities of the business. Val was efficient, had a great personality, and the customers adored and respected her. Little did Ann Marie know that Val didn't like children.

As Val became more and more comfortable in her position, she started making her feelings about Anthony's presence known in the salon. "Ann Marie," she would say, "you have a problem here. Anthony's getting in the way again." At other times she would ask, "Wouldn't he be happier at a day care, where he could spend the whole day with other children and not grown women? I hate to say it, but he's creating a lot of problems for you here." Prior to Val's hiring, there were never any complaints about Anthony.

Ann Marie was conflicted. She even began to believe Val's view that children had no business in the workplace and started looking into day-care facilities. But she wasn't really comfortable with the idea of banishing her son. As she thought the problem through, she began to put everything together.

"Anthony wasn't the problem. In fact, before Val came into the picture, he was well behaved and friendly. The staff enjoyed his antics, and the clients liked to hear him babble on about cartoons and dinosaurs. Val wasn't a team player. The other staff viewed Anthony as part of the salon, not as a 'problem.' If Anthony was doing something he shouldn't be doing, the other manicurists would correct him in a motherly way. There used to be a running joke in the salon. Whenever a new customer would ask who Anthony's mother was, all of the manicurists would say in unison, 'I am.' Anthony was a common thread that kept all of us stitched together—the staff and the clients. He's a conversation piece, sort of a team mascot. Anthony was never referred to as my 'problem' until Val came along.

"It was hard, but I asked Val to leave. And although it took a while, my life and my business are back in order. When I put things into place, I realized that Anthony is the reason why I got into my own business in the first place. I even built a playroom for him in the salon. He belongs there more than Val ever did."

Val's view of Anthony unbalanced her and made the business's owner question herself. Someone who is not a team player can disrupt to the business and will create problems where none exist. Creating an environment that lends itself to making *each* employee feel like an integral part of the business will make them all the more committed. How balanced and in control we feel in the environment can be the scale that allows us to gauge when something has gone wrong.

So if there's a problem in any aspect of your holistic life, you are not in balance. Ann Marie was lucky to figure out where her holistic scale was off-kilter before it created any really serious problems. Val had knocked Ann Marie's life out of balance by not being a team player and by attempting to adversely affect the interconnectedness of Ann Marie's life, mainly Anthony and her business.

✦ THOUGHT TO THINK ON ✦

The entrepreneur who succeeds has a winning team.

Insights into Team Players

1. Your business team, like a sports team, will equate their success to the rest of the team.
2. When an employee says, "*You* have a problem" instead of "*We* have a problem," you can be sure that he or she is not part of the team.
3. Team play in your business is crucial to helping you keep your balance.

THE MIND IS A POWERFUL TOOL

When you get out of bed in the morning, what do you do? Immediately reach for the morning paper and turn on television or radio news? Do you begin to worry about the world before you've had a chance to awaken completely? Many people gravitate toward world problems instantly upon awaking by immediately tuning into the news before they've had a chance to tune into themselves. I admit it's easier to focus our attention on the problems of the world than to analyze our own situations. It is easier yet to identify solutions that we think will work for the world's problems than to search for solutions to our own.

I am not suggesting that you ignore outside stimuli; I *am* suggesting that you reserve that time right before sleep and right after for yourself. Spend it with your inner world. Make up your own television shows or radio broadcast—about you! Instead of concentrating on other people, over whom you have no control, concentrate on yourself. Explore the essence of who you are.

Every night as a child I lulled myself to sleep by visualizing where I wanted to be. My grandmother called it daydreaming or vivid imagination. I was just using the opportunity to live in an imaginary world en route to sleep. And whatever I imagined the night before was right there in my mind when I awakened.

When I operated my business from home, my nighttime ritual included envisioning myself as a successful businesswoman in a nice office. Guess what! It happened!

Give it a try! You can begin to program your mind for prosperity. You'll imprint the path that you will need to follow in order to fulfill your desires. You can dispel any negative thoughts and emotions that would otherwise become roadblocks. Once you understand who you are and where you want to be, start to visualize yourself achieving what you want.

The mind is a very powerful tool; we must try to harness its power to guide our development. We have heard the adage Seeing is believing; so is visualizing. If we can visualize the goals that we wish to attain and believe that we can indeed attain them, we will.

✦ THOUGHT TO THINK ON ✦

All thoughts which have been given feeling and mixed with faith begin immediately to translate themselves into their physical equivalent or counterpart.

—Napoleon Hill

Insights into the Mind as a Powerful Tool

1. Before you jump out of bed in the morning, practice tuning in when you first open your eyes. Spend those first few minutes visualizing things they way you would like them to be.
2. Drift off to your sleep with images in your mind of your goals and wishes.
3. Visualization can help you grow and develop the kind of business that you want.

WRAP-UP

Let's revisit what we've discussed in this chapter. We've explored holistic living and the importance of having a zest for life. We have discussed the importance of loving yourself by implementing a routine to start your day, as a beginning to living a life of balance. We have identified some of the warning signs indicating when your life is out of balance. We've learned that hard work does not always equal success and that finding that quiet place within and contemplation lead to success and achievement. We've also looked at simplifying your life and relieving yourself of excess baggage. We have visited the idea of having a premise, the main idea of your life, and how it works. We now have a better idea of what happiness can look like and a few places where we can find it, and how inner stillness and using the tools of the mind can make our businesses much stronger. We've also discovered the significance of teamwork and what it means to the harmony and balance in our businesses and our lives. These steps take time to cultivate and incorporate in your life. Is it as simple as reciting a mantra over and over? Of course not. Running a business, raising a family, and maintaining a marriage are difficult acts and difficult work. But by viewing your business and private life as one complete event, you will be better able to focus on that which is important to you. Maybe your drive involves your family, or perhaps you want to build a successful business and achieve fame.

Whatever it is, the same rules apply. Decide what having it *all* really means to you, and make your choices accordingly.

REVIEW

Give yourself the gift of self-love.

Again, **identify** and remember your premise.

Keep things in perspective; keep the **scales balanced;** otherwise your "lifeblood" will be depleted.

Simplify your life.

Take time to become a witness to your actions and behavior.

Explore that quiet place within.

Know the importance of teamwork.

Give yourself the gift of visualization.

Chapter 6

EXPANDING YOUR HORIZONS

✦

At long last I felt that I could catch my breath. I understood and practiced the significance of being mindful. I knew that there would always be obstacles, but I also knew that I could overcome them. The travel company was doing fine. I had established a great support system. And with the help of a great spiritual teacher, I was able to achieve balance in my life. All seemed perfect, and I was set for life; at least I thought so. A trip to the local shopping center with my friend Jean soon left me doubting this feeling.

Jean and I enjoyed making things by hand, so when a new arts-and-crafts store opened in the local shopping center, we were among the first to arrive. One of the perks of the opening was that if you made a purchase of ten dollars or more, you were entitled to a free palm reading. Jean was excited about having her palm read. She made her purchase and quickly scurried over to the table for the palm reading while I continued to browse. After her reading, she was elated and insisted that I, too, get one. I wasn't interested. As I passed the reader's table on my way toward the exit, our eyes made contact. He appeared to be no more than twenty years old and looked a lot like Ben Kingsley in his role as the young Mahatma Gandhi. He smiled and started to speak in a quiet voice. "I would like to read your palm; no money is needed. Sit." Jean, in her excitement, started pushing me toward the seat that stood in front of the young man's table. She whispered, "You're going to love this; he is so good."

I sat down and noticed that beside the palm reader was a paperback book entitled *The Beginner's Guide to Palm Reading.* I was skeptical. He looked at both of my palms, then turned my hands over to look at the other sides. Then he turned back to my palm and gently laid my hands down on his table. He picked up his how-to book and started turning pages. He would read a page or two and look at my palms; this went on for about ten minutes. He finally spoke: "What would you like to know? Do you have a special question?" Without thinking, the first thing that blurted out of my mouth was "When will I get married?" He studied my hands again and answered, "When you are in your mid-thirties, not before. See, it says so right here." He pointed to a line in my palm. I thought, This guy is crazy. Whoever heard of not getting married until you're in your thirties? He then said, "Do you have more questions?" I told him that I had heard enough and reached down to the floor to pick up my bag. He reached again for my hand. He said that it was important to get all the questions out of the way so that when he begins to read one's palms, the participant will be able to listen closely to him instead of interrupting to ask their unanswered questions. I sat back in the chair, and he started his reading.

"Okay, if you have no more questions for me, then I would like to read what I see in your palms. I see two very important things. One is that you will do well in your career. And two is that everything that you get from this life you will have to earn." I asked him to explain what he meant. This certainly didn't sound like my idea of fortune-telling. "It's simple," he said matter-of-factly. "No one will die and leave you rich, and you won't marry a wealthy man." I must have looked confused. "This is not such a problem; you seem to have a good start. All you have to do is gather information, turn it into knowledge, apply that knowledge in your life, and from that will come the wisdom to know what to do or not to do. And all will go very well, and you will grow."

When Jean and I got back to my apartment, she was still glowing from whatever the palm reader had told her. I was less enthusiastic. I asked her, "How can you believe someone that is reading a how-to book on palm reading while reading your palms?" "Why not?" she said. "That's exactly what you're doing. People call you to make reservations to places that you've never heard of, and you manage to get it together for them by using how-to books."

I thought about the palm reader's predictions and concluded that his message was that I was to be self-sufficient. I would have to work for whatever I was to become. What an inspiration this was. To travel the path to self-sufficiency, I would have to learn, gain knowledge, and develop myself. That led me to the sixth process of entrepreneurial success—**EXPANDING YOUR HORIZONS.**

EXPANDING THE COMFORT ZONE

Think about your first day of school. You were probably five or six years old. It was most likely scary for you to go off to a strange place for the whole day. You were leaving your mom, your toys, your room, all the things you knew. However, you needed to take this step to learn.

When you headed off to school that very first time, you were stepping outside your comfort zone and into a different world. Maybe you cried. Maybe you thought you'd hate it. But eventually you adapted to your surroundings; you grew a little bit. And then you began to feel comfortable again.

A comfort zone is that part of your life that is familiar. When you step outside of that space, you expand your comfort zone.

In my life, I have repeated that experience many times so that I could learn and grow. Leaving your comfort zone is as important at age thirty, forty, or fifty as it was when you were five. And it's scary every single time. I remember a time when I was frightened at the thought of speaking to a group of three people and decided that if I wanted to get corporate or convention business, I would need to learn how to address small groups. Subsequently, I enrolled in public-speaking classes. It was terrifying for me to go to those classes at first. But I put myself through it and forced myself to broaden my horizons. As a result, I became a much better speaker. Actually, I'm a better person because of it.

Those speaking courses allowed me to put myself out there in a way that I couldn't before. I'm not suggesting that there's not a little nervousness when I walk out in front of a group, but a newly developed confidence also exists.

I started by standing in front of twelve or fourteen people in a speaking course, and now I am comfortable addressing audiences of thousands. That kind of expansion is something that happens gradually. Expanding your comfort zone is accomplished by taking small steps. Once you do something that had frightened you and you see that you were able to accomplish the task and avoid disaster, you will be less hesitant to take the next small step and then the next. Once you begin expanding your horizons, you will never want to stop. And if you want to grow in business, you must grow as a person. If I had not overcome my fear of public speaking, I would never have been able to take my business to the next level.

Expanding your comfort zone has everything to do with how confident you feel in any endeavor. Self-development helps you feel more confident. When nervousness is built on lack of self-confidence, then it makes your life extremely uncomfortable.

We have to broaden our comfort zone in many different ways. I think about my sister-in-law Margo, who was really on a mission to broaden and improve her life. Shortly after she and my brother married, my husband and I took them out to dinner. I asked her if she would like to order the wine. She said that she would be delighted to do so. She took the wine list and studied it for a few minutes. Then she ordered an excellent vintage. I said, "If that's what you want, that's what we're going to get. But how did you know about that particular wine? Have you spent time studying wines?" She confided in me that in the past she had been so intimidated by the thought of having to order wine that the mere thought of it had actually ruined her appetite. She decided to take a wine course. Now she actually looked forward to discussing the subject of wine.

I was impressed. It showed me that people can get knowledge and information in so many places to improve their lives—perhaps through a course, a novel, or a movie on television. You have to be open and receptive to information from all sorts of places. Take classes, read books, talk to people. Everything helps.

✦ **THOUGHT TO THINK ON** ✦

An improved quality of life can be obtained through unexpected sources and for unexpected reasons. Stay open.

Insights into Expanding Your Comfort Zone

1. Realize what your "comfort zone" is.
2. Decide if you're ready to expand that comfort zone.
3. Understand that expanding your comfort zone gives you self-confidence.
4. Expanding your comfort zone prepares you for expanding your business and personal life.

STRETCHING YOUR ZONE

As you begin to expand your business, you must constantly assess what you need to learn and experience. Starting out in the travel business, I knew that I needed to speak effectively in public, deal with a diverse client population, and learn to expand the scope of my travel services.

When I took my first group on a plane trip to the theater in New York City, I was only seventeen and had spent the previous year and a half selling people bus tours; I suddenly found myself with sixteen people waiting to take an escorted air tour to the "big city." I was terrified, but I needed to look like I was in control. I needed to be as professional and efficient as possible. I knew that to expand my business I would need to be comfortable on airplanes. Therefore, about ten days before the trip, I took a ride out to the airport and walked around to get acquainted with the area. A couple of days later, I went to the ticket counter where I would be checking my group in, introduced myself to the reservation agent, and explained my dilemma. The agent called for a supervisor to give me the grand tour of the airport and explained every step that I would go through with the group, from checking in and getting seat assignments to claiming their luggage as a group once we arrived in New York. Finally, the supervisor made arrangements for me to go aboard an airplane and talk with a pilot. My comfort zone was stretched a little further that day. I had faced my fears and concerns and had taken positive steps to alleviate them. I made certain that I was prepared for the trip I had scheduled. The trip was a success, and I gained the confidence that I needed to expand the scope of my business.

It is easy to become complacent or to be paralyzed by your fear and anxiety. In business as in life, you have to constantly expand your experience and knowledge. If you are not moving ahead, then you are losing ground.

When I look back on my life, I've been in constant movement. Many people have asked me, "How did you feel at sixteen or seventeen years of age selling people vacations?" Well, I thought that it was the natural thing to do. I grew up in a family where work was the order of the day. At ten you sell newspapers, at fourteen you do yard work for the neighbors and wash cars, and at seventeen you do something else. I had constantly expanded my comfort zone by taking small steps until at seventeen I felt comfortable calling people on the phone and convincing them to take a trip. Then one day somebody said, "We want to experience a plane trip." To accommodate the client, I had to stretch a little further. Sometimes you can predict the small steps that you must take, and sometimes you are forced into them. I never knew then what the client wanted when the phone rang, and I don't know now. But whatever it is, if I want to be successful, I've got to be ready to learn and grow.

I believe that you should grow and expand by taking very small steps. As the old saying goes, Inch by inch, it's a cinch. Growth and expansion don't always require giant steps. Nor is it always possible to take them. It's little steps that get you where you want to go. If you take it step-by-step, before you know it, you've walked a thousand miles. I know because it happened to me.

In the beginning of my career, a lady who had heard about my bus trips called to find out if we could arrange for her a package tour to Europe. Of course, I said yes. I told her that all she needed to do was tell me what she wanted and I would call her back later that day. She wanted to visit the Vatican, the Coliseum, the Forum, and the Palatine. She had been told by friends that she shouldn't miss the Catacombs of St. Sebastian or the Via Veneto. My head was spinning as I thought to myself, Where on earth are these places? I thought that she might give me a hint if I asked her what hotel she would like to stay in. Her answer was "Someplace nice, dear, near the Spanish Steps." The Spanish Steps, I thought. Maybe these things are in Spain. "Oh, and by the way, I *must* see Michelangelo's *David*." I was clueless! Who on earth was this Michael person? I told her that in order to provide her with the best itinerary I could, I would need two days to get back to her with information. Not one thing she mentioned rang a bell from my high school classes. I looked around the room at the other women who were on the phone selling bus trips and asked them if they had ever heard of these places. They hadn't!

I managed to find all the information that I needed by using the library, calling folks, and looking through every travel book that I could find. The lady took the trip, enjoyed herself, and best of all, referred other people to me. And I had expanded my frame of reference.

✦ THOUGHT TO THINK ON ✦

They know enough who know how to learn.

—Henry Brooks Adams

Insights into Stretching the Zone

1. Constantly assess what you need to learn and experience.
2. Take positive steps to alleviate your fears and concerns.

3. Growth usually comes in small steps.
4. Sometimes you can predict the small steps; sometimes you take them out of necessity.
5. If you are not moving forward, then you are falling behind.

EXPANDING YOUR FRAME OF REFERENCE

Growing as a person involves expanding your frame of reference, the sum total of all your experience and learning. Think of it as a big picture frame. Within its borders are all the things you know, can do, are aware of, and think about. If you were to remain in that frame for the rest of your life, you would be the same person twenty years from now. You will have spent your entire adult life thinking, talking, and experiencing the same finite number of things. As an entrepreneur and a human being, your approach to life should be more expansive than that. Push out the walls of your frame on a regular basis. Choose a new path to take, someone new to meet, a different way of thinking about yourself and the world. Expanding my frame of reference has served me well in both my business and my private life. I was raised in a lower-middle-class, blue-collar, inner-city family. We were a meatloaf-and-mashed-potatoes kind of family. I wouldn't have known a lobster if it had crawled onto my plate. But as I grew my company, I knew that I would need to know more about the world if I intended to deal with a variety of clients. One thing that I did was to enroll in cooking classes to learn about fine cuisine and the art of entertaining. As a result, the ability to host both formal *and* informal dinner parties has brought me additional clients. Moreover, I've organized group cooking and dining tours in various places around the world, which has also increased my business.

I realized early on that I needed to broaden my frame of reference. First, when I wanted more business, I knew I had to leave my comfort zone and gain, step-by-step, the knowledge that I needed to be able to offer my clients the type of travel packages that they desired.

In order to expand my business and offer all types of vacation packages, I had to know something about where I was sending my clients so that I could respond to their questions and needs.

You broaden your frame of reference by focusing in on how and why you need particular knowledge. In my case, I knew that I needed to learn about some of the places that I was sending my clients. For instance, if somebody wanted to go to Gettysburg, I read up on it so that I could have a more informed opinion. When possible, I visited the place myself so that I would have firsthand knowledge.

When I wanted to be a better parent, I read books on child development. When I couldn't sort out the ideas in the books, I consulted with professionals and other married people.

✦ THOUGHT TO THINK ON ✦

I am not afraid of storms, for I am learning how to sail my ship.
—Louisa May Alcott

Insights into Frame of Reference

1. Your frame of reference is the sum total of your learning and experience.
2. Growing as a person involves expanding your frame of reference.
3. Expanding your frame of reference is accomplished by leaving your comfort zone and acquiring the knowledge and ability needed to allow you and your business to grow.

GATHERING KNOWLEDGE

Life is about gathering knowledge. You must use every resource that you can get your hands on to learn about the world. When you stop learning, you stop living. Some people feel that once they finish their formal education, learning stops. The world is constantly changing, as is our business. New technology and new sources of information require constant updating of our skills and knowledge. To stop learning is to fall behind and drop by the wayside. You must constantly enrich your life and your skills if you are to be successful and fulfilled. Answer the questions that follow to acquaint yourself with the issues involved in gathering knowledge:

Knowledge Exercise

1. What subjects will expand your horizons? (For example, learning a foreign language, learning a computer-software program, etc.)

2. What kind of things do you enjoy doing? (What type of movies do you like to watch? What do you like to do on weekends?)

3. How many hours a week do you spend doing these things? _____ Do any of them help you advance toward your goals?

4. What type of information gathering do you like to do? (Surfing the Internet, reading magazines, watching news shows?)

As we can see from this exercise, we all have many interests. Some of them are personal and enrich our lives; others are related to our effort to advance in order to meet our goals. Still others can serve both purposes. We must decide how to balance these interests to meet our goals while still enriching our lives.

The exercise also illustrates the wide range of information sources that are available to us in the information age. We must also be able to choose which sources of knowledge and information to access without overloading ourselves. Today there is an unprecedented number of sources that we can access to enrich our lives.

There are many traditional methods of learning, including books written about any subject that we may wish to study. There are courses and seminars that are independently run or part of college curriculums, and others that are available on tape and video. In addition, with the arrival of the personal computer, there is a new, unlimited source of knowledge literally at our fingertips. Almost any subject can be accessed through the use of computer discs and CDs. The Internet makes an abundance of information available to everyone right in their own homes.

Keep in mind that, regardless of the source, what is important is to gain knowledge in those areas that will enhance and improve our lives, bring balance and harmony to them, and help us run our businesses more efficiently. We all have to make a living, and as businesspeople we have to continue to learn new things every day that will enhance our business and allow it to grow. Given this, we should enjoy the process of continued learning.

There is an old saying that Knowledge is power, but the real power is being able to use your knowledge to improve your life. It is important to be happy with your decisions and therefore with your life. It is also important to be able to turn your knowledge into a tool that you can use to better yourself. It is not important or necessary to absorb data like an encyclopedia or a computer. It is important that you do know how to find needed information and then to be able to turn it into actions that will open doors and propel you toward your goals. That is what makes knowledge powerful. Let's take a look at Dave's story:

Dave's Story

When Dave opened up his first hobby shop ten years ago, his plan was to have a small business. He was close to retirement, and he thought his business would provide a nice supplemental income while allowing him to do something he enjoyed.

As it turned out, several of Dave's customers wanted to collect old Lionel trains, which he knew little about. At the time,

Dave wasn't interested in them, nor did he feel like paying a great deal of money for them. But he thought about it for several weeks and decided to take a class at the local community college on antique trains.

Much to Dave's surprise, he loved the class and developed a real interest in antique trains. Dave took the knowledge that he acquired and began collecting a few pieces. They all sold instantly.

Dave took the information that he learned in the course and used it to expand his business in a profitable direction, since Lionel trains are a very popular collector's item. Before he took the class, Dave had no idea how large a market there was for this product. With his newfound knowledge he was able to increase his number of customers and his profits. He was eventually able to open another hobby shop and continues to be quite successful. Without his interest in broadening his knowledge, he would not have been able to expand his business into this profitable area.

So you see, a little bit of knowledge *can* go a long way. It's what you choose to do with the knowledge that matters. Until you can use information effectively, it's just data that may or may not have any value. It becomes valuable when we use it to advance our interests. In my case, I gathered the information that I needed for my New York trip and turned it into what I call a knowledge unit. It helped me move my business forward. The trip was so successful that six of the initial sixteen travelers signed on immediately. The others told people how wonderful it was. So is knowledge powerful? In this case it was.

✦ THOUGHT TO THINK ON ✦

Knowledge is power. Know where to find it and know how to use it.

Insights into Gathering Knowledge

1. Life is about gathering knowledge.
2. You must constantly enrich your life and skills if you are to be successful and fulfilled.
3. Power is being able to use your knowledge to better yourself as a businessperson.

INFORMATION OVERLOAD

We are a society that is subjected to information overload. It's coming at us from all directions—television, radio, newspapers and magazines, and the Internet are all at our fingertips. It is important to be able to filter through all this information and determine what will make your business move forward.

When I started, there were no computers and no Internet. I had to sift through libraries and encyclopedias. Yet I was able to take my limited resources and turn that information into knowledge that I could use. My point is, it doesn't matter how many resources you have; it's what you do with the information that counts.

It is to your advantage as an entrepreneur to understand and use technology to enhance your business. Technology can be the most important asset to any entrepreneur. Computers, E-mail, the Internet, web sites, and fax machines have changed the nature of business and gathering knowledge dramatically.

A successful business depends on the transfer of information and the gathering of knowledge. Never has doing so been easier. Computers make tasks that once took many tedious hours of repetitious work almost instantaneous. We can respond to our customers' wants and needs more quickly, more completely, and with fewer errors. Computers can also provide us with educational resources, from up-to-date encyclopedias to at-home learning programs, never before available. Computers give us access to E-mail as well. With E-mail and faxes, we can communicate quickly, giving us the ability to reach out to the entire world and making it possible to give our clients information and services that were never before available. Computers also give us access to the Internet. The Internet is the greatest source of knowledge that was ever conceived. You can literally find information on any subject that interests you or that you need for your business. It also provides web sites, letting us advertise our business to people throughout the world at a cost that is much less than conventional advertising. Let's see what the Internet did for Joanne.

Joanne's Story

Joanne loved to travel and over the years had accumulated an extensive collection of art objects and jewelry from the places she had visited. She had become quite knowledgeable and often advised friends on the finer points of collecting. She was constantly being asked to shop for these friends on her travels and never failed to please them with her selections. She often thought of opening her own business but felt that there were simply too many obstacles to overcome; finding a business site, marketing, and accumulating inventory all seemed too much for her to handle.

She discovered the Internet and enjoyed visiting web pages dealing with those countries that reflected her travels. One day, while she was showing her collection to a friend, she confessed to her dream of going into business. When her friend asked her why she didn't, she explained her reservations. Sharing her passion for the Internet, the friend asked her if she had ever thought about designing her own web page and selling over the Internet. She already had access to the Internet, and it would be a simple matter to obtain space for a web site.

Thinking about the idea, she decided to give it a try. She knew nothing about creating a web page, so she hired a professional who designed an attractive site, including graphics and descriptions of the products that Joanne collected. Using

E-mail and contacts found on other web sites, she was able to locate merchandisers who were willing to forward products directly to her customers, filling her orders. Working from her home, Joanne became more successful than she could have imagined. Her business grew rapidly, and she eventually serviced customers thoughout the world. Using the Internet and her own web site, she was able to become successful doing something that she loved.

Joanne, and many others, have found that the Internet has been their path to success, enabling them to market their products and services and in many instances, like Joanne, even running thriving businesses from their homes.

As wonderful a tool for entrepreneurs as the Internet has become, as with any innovation, there can be a downside to this technology. Due to the massive volume of information that can be accessed, it is possible to become a victim of information overload.

We cannot, however, become lost in this limitless source of information. We must still be able to decide what is important to us personally and in our business. We must also be able to put the information that we gather into knowledgeable units that will help to move us forward. My friend Carrie is a good example of what happens when we suffer from information overload. Let's take a look at her story:

Carrie's Story

Carrie spent fifteen years gathering information about aromatherapy, yoga, tai chi, flower essences, health and beauty tips, meditation, sound therapy, massage, homeopathy, and nutrition. She has spent time and money on books, audio- and videotapes, classes, and computer programs. She has spent countless hours on the Internet. And she has spent an equal amount of time talking to experts.

One day I asked Carrie what she intended to do with all of the information. I suggested that she consider starting her own business. She loved the idea but was overwhelmed by the possibilities and had no idea where to start. In fact, Carrie told me that she had been struggling for years to organize the tons of information that she had gathered into a viable business. She simply had too many bits and pieces of information.

I offered to help her organize everything. After several meetings, we finally came up with the perfect business package. It would give her the freedom she wanted for her family and a good income. She was finally able to organize the data by eliminating the overload and concentrating on the knowledge that she would need to launch a successful business.

She now has an all-day workshop designed to relieve stress and tension called "Healing the Whole Person." She also has weekend retreats for families designed to strengthen the bond between them, called "The Nurtured Child."

Carrie also has started writing a syndicated column based on the techniques used in her two programs. Now that Carrie's information is organized knowledge, it is easier for her to be successful in her own business.

This paring down and focusing is essential to your business and your life. The task has become harder in recent years with the proliferation of information, making it all the more essential that you keep only information that is necessary.

✦ THOUGHT TO THINK ON ✦

The will to succeed is important, but what's even more important is the will to prepare.

—Bobby Knight

Insights into Information Overload

1. It is imperative that we determine what information will move our business forward.
2. It is not important how much information you have accumulated but what you do with it.
3. Computers have revolutionized the gathering and dissemination of information and have made tasks that once took many tedious hours almost instantaneous.

ASK QUESTIONS

With all the other sources available, we overlook asking questions as a basic means of gathering information. Somewhere along the line, I decided that I would not be afraid to do so. In school we were often chastised for asking stupid questions. But when you are running a business, there is no such thing. So if I want to know something, I ask.

I have a friend who is a reporter, and we were talking about the art of asking questions. She says that what often happens at news conferences is that the one question that the audience really wants answered is never asked. The reporters inevitably assume that everyone else knows the answer, and they don't want to appear ignorant by asking it themselves. There's a crime reporter in Florida named Edna Buchanan. You might recognize her name because she has gone on to write true crime novels. Edna Buchanan distinguished herself among crime reporters by always asking the questions that nobody else had the nerve to ask. I'm not talking about inappropriate questions. By asking seemingly mundane questions, she accumulated important details and eventually won herself a Pulitzer.

I have found that this happens in my business as well. A necessary piece of information is lost because a question was not asked. So don't be afraid to ask questions. The art of questioning is the most powerful tool that you can have both as an entrepreneur and in your private life. Feel comfortable asking questions and do not make judgments about how others view them. No amount of reference sources will give you knowledge about what is in someone else's mind. You can't successfully run a business without speaking up.

✦ THOUGHT TO THINK ON ✦

There is really nothing more to say—except why. But since why is difficult to handle, one must take refuge in how.
                                        —*Toni Morrison*

Insights into Asking Questions

1. Don't be afraid to ask questions.
2. The art of asking questions is a powerful tool.
3. Your business can't run effectively if you don't speak up.

PAY ATTENTION TO YOUR SURROUNDINGS

Information is all around you. It exists in books, classes, and conversation, on the Internet, and in Mother Nature. It is also present in our surroundings. Reminders of knowledge, wisdom, and information are all around us if we just take the time to pay attention. I have learned so much as a result of observing my surroundings.

Be aware of those around you. Never take people for granted. They are the most important part of your business and must be understood if you are to succeed. Be aware not only of what they say but also of how they say it and what they do. Learn to read the signals that people provide. This is knowledge that cannot be found in books or on the Internet, but is invaluable. Let's take a look at how a conversation helped David prosper:

The Conversation

David hadn't come to his favorite diner to get rich; he came simply to have lunch. But get rich he did. David wa at a table in the diner, waiting for his food to be served. He was lost in thought, trying to decide what he was going to do with his life. He was thinking of getting married and starting a family, which meant that he would soon have additional responsibilities. He worked as a machinist and was a part-time inventor, but he longed for his own business, one in which he could utilize his talents as a designer. As he pondered his future, he could not help but overhear a conversation.

Two men were engaged in a heated discussion at the next table. It became apparent that they were both building contractors. Their discussion became more heated as they began to vent their frustrations. Both were experiencing construction delays due to the lack of availability of parts that they needed to complete their projects. It seemed that every company made their own unique product, and none ever seemed to have the required items in stock. Since parts were not interchangeable, the men had no option but to wait until they could receive the shipment of items that they needed. David, at first only dimly aware of what was being said, began to listen more closely.

David had always pictured himself as the inventor of the next great gizmo, which would bring him fame and fortune. Later, as David thought about the conversation that he had been drawn into hearing, an idea slowly began to take shape in his mind.

Several years have passed, and David is a very successful and wealthy manufacturer. His plant produces standardized hardware for use in construction. His products are designed to work with all other fixtures and hardware. They aren't glamorous, but they are constantly in demand. Being aware of his surroundings, listening to the needs and wants of others, and being able to respond to them set David on his personal road to entrepreneurship.

Pay attention—you never know when or where your next inspiration may come from.

Lastly, as you move throughout your day, pay closer attention to the things that nature has provided to bring joy and balance to your life. The world is filled with wonders; by letting them fill your life and give you added inspiration and motivation, you will become a complete person. The following story will explain what I mean:

The Flight of the Bumblebee

I had just completed a speech and was leaving the ballroom to return to my room when I was approached by a woman who had been in the audience. She introduced herself and proceeded to tell me her story. She removed a striking bumblebee pin that she was wearing and asked if I knew that scientifically it was impossible for a bumblebee to fly. Bumblebees have round, fat bodies and a short wingspan, making them aerodynamically unsuited for flight. I responded that I hadn't known that but found it interesting. The woman continued to say that she wore the pin to remind herself that anything in life is possible if we just believe that it can be achieved and work to accomplish it. Anytime that she felt that her goals were out of reach, she would wear her pin and recall how the bumblebee defies all odds to achieve its goal. She presented me with the pin and thanked me for the positive messages included in my presentation. I still have the pin, and whenever I wear it, I am reminded of how much we can learn from nature if we only take the time to look.

Nature can provide us with many such wonders that can give us much-needed hope when our road to success seems to be strewn with obstacles. So take time to appreciate the natural world for its beauty and for the messages and lessons that it can provide.

> ✦ **THOUGHT TO THINK ON** ✦
>
> *The environment is telling and showing you all you need to know to make you a complete person. Are you watching? Are you listening?*

Insights into Paying Attention

1. Information, messages, and lessons exist everywhere to help us meet our goals.
2. Stay aware! Your next business venture could depend on it.
3. There is much information as well as inspiration that we can find in nature.

WRAP-UP

Let's review where we've been in this discussion on the process of expanding your horizons. We've examined the comfort zone and the importance of moving beyond it. We've talked about expanding your zone by leaving your comfort zone and taking small steps to move beyond your present boundaries. We've discussed expanding your frame of reference, that sum total of your knowledge and experience, and assessing what you must learn for the development of both your business and personal life.

Finally, we've talked about knowledge and how you can turn it into a powerful tool. We've talked about sources of knowledge. We've discussed the promise and the pitfalls of the information society in which we live and the impact of modern technology, from computers and the Internet to the fax machine, and how it can improve your life and your business. We discussed the need to ask questions and to open yourself to other people and to the world's natural wonders.

To grow as a businessperson, you must be willing to identify your weaknesses and then work to improve them. You must be ready to explore the seemingly peripheral subjects that will help you move forward in business.

REVIEW

Expanding your comfort zone will bring about self-confidence.

Your **business grows** as your frame of reference grows.

Knowledge is a lifetime process. Once you stop learning, you stop living.

Accept and use new technology to the advantage of your business.

Organize your knowledge effectively.

If you want to know, **ask!** Don't be afraid to ask questions.

Stay aware and alert to your surroundings and the people around you.

CONCLUSION

In the preceding six chapters I have discussed my life and the lessons that I have learned in becoming an entrepreneur. The path of the entrepreneur is by no means clear. No two people can follow the same path or share the same experiences. What I have tried to do is to give you a general blueprint for success in business as well as in life. Being an entrepreneur involves more than making a living; it is making a life. I have cited numerous examples of people who have also worked to make themselves successful and fulfilled. To be a success you must find that which will fulfill your personal needs as well as that which will give you the tools to accomplish your goals in business.

I send you my best wishes in all you do and hope that this book provides some of the tools and guidance along the way.